The Indomitable
Francis H. Cook of Spokane

The Indomitable
Francis H. Cook of Spokane

A Man of Vision

by Doris J. Woodward

TORNADO CREEK
PUBLICATIONS

Tony and Suzanne Bamonte
P.O. Box 8625
Spokane, Washington 99203
(509) 838-7114, Fax (509) 455-6798
www.tornadocreekpublications.com

First edition published 2010
by Tornado Creek Publications

Printed by Marquette Books of Spokane, Washington
www.MarquetteBooks.com

ISBN: 978-0-9821529-1-1
ISSN (*Pacific Northwesterner*): 0030-882X
Library of Congress Control Number: 2010941123

Cover photo:
Postcard image of how Mirror Lake in Manito Park appeared around the time
Francis H. Cook owned the property, courtesy Bill Stewart.

Photo Credits

Photos credited "Cook Family" have been shared by family members, in particular Francis Cook's great-granddaughters, Jan Edmonds (granddaughter of Frank Arthur Cook) and Laura Poulin (granddaughter of Ralph Wheeler Cook).

Photos from the collection at the Eastern Washington State Historical Society/ Northwest Museum of Arts & Culture and are noted as **MAC**.

Other credits are as noted in the photo captions.

Table of Contents

From the Author

Finishing this book about Francis H. Cook and his wife, Laura, has caused me to reflect on some of my previous work. Although I had a background in journalism and the printing industry, I didn't begin writing until late in life and, once started, it hasn't seemed to stop. I have now completed four fairly major projects, and they have all been about interesting men, who each made their own unique mark on the pages of history.

Doris J. Woodward, 2010

- The first was a lengthy article for the National Genealogical Society Quarterly, which was entitled "The Fletcher Legends." It was primarily the story of my great-grandfather, Matthew Fletcher, an inventor and engineer who came from Birmingham, England, married and had children in Vienna, Austria, and eventually brought his burgeoning family to Louisville, Kentucky—an interesting man by any standards.

- The second was an account of General Thomas Tannatt, Civil War soldier and a man who was influential in the early years of Eastern Washington, especially in Walla Walla, Whitman College, Farmington and Spokane.

- The third was the story of Harper Joy, a Walla Walla boy who, with sheer guts and determination, made a name for himself in Spokane as an astute securities salesman and a part-time circus clown, a man well-beloved by everyone who knew him.

- The fourth is this work on Francis H. Cook, an important figure in early Spokane life, who was constantly thinking of new ventures and new avenues to explore.

Thinking back on these four men, it is fascinating for me to realize they had one thing very much in common. Each of them had a wife who was interesting, intelligent, ahead of her time, and worthy of being written about in her own right. I think perhaps it was this fact that made my research and work on these stories so worthwhile. I pause to think about my great-grandmother Leocadia Dědek, a Bohemian girl who was a musician and embroiderer, whose talents were passed on to my mother and other members of the family. I recall Elizabeth Tappan, a young lady from Massachusetts who married her handsome beau from West Point, Thomas Tannatt. It was her life-long correspondence with her family that helped immeasurably with my research. I knew Dorothy Mendenhall Joy, Harper's wife, as she lived next door to me here in Spokane. Dorothy Joy came from a fine Spokane family and was a strong and intelligent woman—an excellent match for her popular and gregarious husband.

Now I have the pleasure of introducing Laura McCarty Cook, certainly one of the exceptional women of her time, a woman who supported her husband through the best and worst of times and provided a mother's love and care for their eleven children.

Doris J. Woodward, 2010

(Sketch by Don Neraas)

Acknowledgements

With grateful appreciation, I would like to thank the following who have assisted me in one way or another to complete this book:

- Rose Krause and Jane Davey, Archives, Eastern Washington State Historical Society/Northwest Museum of Arts & Culture (MAC). They are always willing to help find that special picture or map that is available nowhere else.
- Laura Arksey, for her knowledge and expertise, which are so vitally important to Spokane researchers, and for her excellent proofreading.
- Riva Dean at the Northwest Room, Spokane Public Library, who is always willing to help in the search for maps, books, and any Spokane history.
- Eastern Washington State Digital Archives, Cheney, Washington.
- Ancestry.com for providing online all of the U.S. Censuses from 1790 to 1930, which proved to be so essential in researching the families of Francis Cook and Laura McCarty.
- To Jan Edmonds, Laura Poulin, Lolita "Corky" Fuson, and Burton Alvis, all descendants of Francis and Laura Cook who provided photographs and family memories. Jan and Laura also who very helpful in proofreading and editing copy.
- To Louis Livingston, who many years ago interviewed three of the Cook children, and to John Ellingson, who transcribed those interviews. These oral histories have been instrumental in furnishing important Cook family information that would have been otherwise lost.

I would be remiss if I failed to express my appreciation to my friends and publishers, Suzanne and Tony Bamonte, who provided most of the resource material on Francis Cook. Besides this, they have always given their support and assistance when research is tough and prospects discouraging. A special "thank you" to Tony, for urging me to take on this challenge. It has been an adventure for me!

Foreword

In the past, two people were especially instrumental in researching the genealogy of the Cook family. One was Warren L. Cook, PhD, the son of Silas Warren Cook and therefore a grandson of Francis Cook. Warren taught history and anthropology at Castleton College in Vermont and worked on Francis Cook's genealogy for many years. In Oregon, 3,000 miles west, Eva O. Cook was also researching the Cook family. She was a descendant of Francis's uncle, Major Wesley Cook, the brother of Francis's father, Silas. Major Wesley was Eva's grandfather, whose son, John Wesley, was Eva's father. Eva and Warren began their research during the 1960s. Through a contact with the Washington County Chapter of the Ohio Genealogical Society at Marietta, Warren and Eva were introduced, and for the next three decades, research was shared between the two of them and with Eva's son, Col. Wesley A. Cook.

Those of us researching the Cook families owe a debt of gratitude to these three people, who diligently gathered information and saved it for future generations in a time before computers and the Internet. They were able to trace our allied families back to the 1760s and possibly 150 years earlier. We not only benefited from the Cook lineage, but were also given short biographies on many of our ancestors.

If you have any information to share on the Johnson Cook ancestors or descendants, please contact:

Timothy Cook
25376 Lynford Street
Farmington Hills, Michigan 48336

Janet Edmonds
10067 S.E. 213th Place
Kent, Washington 98031

Caroline C. Hennessy
P.O. Box 1063
Burns, Oregon 97220

Jan Edmonds
Great granddaughter of
Francis and Laura Cook

Introducing
Francis H. Cook

(Photo courtesy Cook family)

His life was gentle, and the elements
So mix'd in him that Nature might stand up
And say to all the world, "This was a man!"

(Shakespeare)

The road to the top of Mount Spokane winds upwards from Highway 2, through Green Bluff, twisting and turning as it climbs up the beautiful mountain that graces the northeast Spokane skyline. Even today it is not an easy road to drive. Its destination is near the top of the largest mountain in the Spokane area, the southernmost mountain of the Selkirk Range.

Evidence indicates Native Americans occupied the mountain in early times, for hunting game and collecting berries, and may have used it for spiritual purposes as well. It was naturally of interest to the first white Spokane settlers, but its later development and importance to the area were due almost entirely to the vision of one man, Francis H. Cook, an energetic and highly motivated early Spokanite. He is fondly called the "Father of Mount Spokane State Park," but that happened almost twenty years after he arrived in Spokane and was not his initial purpose for coming to Spokane.

Francis Cook was a remarkable man of many accomplishments. His story is, in many ways, typical of the early settlers and business tycoons of the Inland Northwest and other areas of the United States, but his ambition and versatility went far beyond that of the ordinary businessman—resulting in major contributions to Spokane and the surrounding area that are in evidence even today, 130 years later. He gained much of his early experience in Iowa and other parts of the United States, eventually moving to coastal Washington, where he was a printer and publisher. He was elected to serve on the state legislature and chosen to be its president. He was one of the most important advocates for the Spokane area, and it was during his legislative term that Spokane County was created. In 1879 he left the coast and came to Spokane, where he remained for the rest of his life.

Any account of Francis Cook's life involves much of Spokane's early history—the *Spokan Times*, the first motorized street railway, Manito Park, the Little Spokane River and the lake at Wandermere, plus the final *coup de grâce*, the development of Mount Spokane.

The following narrative describes the variety of enterprises Francis Cook embraced—writing, printing, publishing, land developing, farming, and building. Of even more importance, we find that Francis Cook was a good father and husband and an honorable man, who had the strength of his convictions. In this publication we will study Francis and his wife, Laura McCarty, and their life together in Spokane.

In Appendix I, we provide information about their heritage, as Francis and Laura were both descendants of Washington pioneer families. Appendix II is devoted to the eleven Cook children, an interesting and diverse group of individuals. Appendix III gives insight into Francis H. Cook, the author. He was a prolific writer, particularly in the field of journalism, but he also had a distinctive flair for words and enjoyed writing about a variety of subjects.

Some early accounts of Francis Cook contain many questions and several errors. Hopefully, some of these will be resolved in the following pages. The accumulation of historical data is an ongoing project, and there is always the possibility of finding further evidence of events that happened over 100 years ago.

Section I
Life in Western Washington

The Early Years

In the spring of 1871, a young man ended a year-long journey at Steilacoom, Washington, a small town near Olympia, Washington. He was twenty years old, tall and good-looking, and was hoping to find work. His name was Francis Henry Cook. He was a printer by trade and had begun the trip working as an apprentice printer from Iowa to New York to San Francisco. The end of the journey in Steilacoom proved to be the beginning of his lifelong love affair with the Pacific Northwest.

Francis Cook was born in Marietta, Washington County, Ohio, in 1851. He and his twin brother, Franklin Pierce Cook, were the third and fourth sons of Silas and Catharine Wheeler Cook (it is not known which twin was born first). Their parents were both from families that had settled early in Marietta, and father Silas was known in town as an engineer. What he did to warrant that title is not known, but in a town like Marietta there would have been a huge need for men with mechanical abilities, as the town was noted for ship and canal building, boiler manufacturing and other businesses requiring engineers and machinists.

In the 1860 U.S. Census, Silas and Catharine are found with seven children—six sons: Frederick J., Lucian F., Franklin P., Francis H., Joseph S., and Charles A.; and one daughter: Mary L. By 1863, although Silas was successful in Ohio, according to their son Charles, his father and mother and their sizable family "were eager to see what was in the wild and woolly West."

Their sights were set on Iowa, still a relatively unsettled state, although there was a large enough population to have furnished a sizable number of troops to serve in the Civil War. According to Francis Cook's wife, Laura, who many years later described her husband's trip to Iowa, his family's destination was Council Bluffs in Pottawattamie County on the far western side of the state, across the Missouri River from Omaha, Nebraska. The question arises as to why they chose this far-away place in Iowa as their destination. We find that Catharine's younger sister, Lavina, had previously moved to Iowa with her physician husband, Frank Clarke. Catharine's older brother, Henry, had also located in western Iowa and was practicing law in Van Buren Township, later becoming a judge. It appears these relatives were instrumental in encouraging the Cooks to follow them to Iowa.

According to Laura Cook, the family left Marietta in the spring of 1863, when Francis was twelve years old. The journey took six weeks and covered a distance of 1,000 miles. They traveled about ten miles per day. Some of the family rode in wagons, but the older boys walked most of the way—having a grand time swimming, hunting, fishing and providing food. There were, according to Charles Cook, "plenty of eats and of the very best."

The Cooks remained in Iowa for thirteen years, during which time they moved to Magnolia in Harrison County, just north of Pottawattamie County. According to Laura Cook, Francis learned the printing trade as a young boy, when he was hired to work in the office of the *Harrison County Union*, a paper owned and edited by Judge Henry Ford, Catharine's brother and therefore Francis's uncle. It was the beginning of Francis Cook's ongoing association with journalism. Printing was his first real vocation and one he espoused for many years. At age sixteen, he and another young man purchased the *Union* and published it for a year and a half.

Francis wanted an education, however, and selling his interest in the paper, in September 1868 he enrolled in the State University of Iowa in Iowa City.

Francis H. Cook
(Photo courtesy Cook family)

He found no special course was offered for a journalist and was refused admittance unless he took a regular course. Francis was disappointed but informed the university authorities he would remain until they allowed him to take the courses he desired. His request was granted after he returned every day for two weeks. This kind of determination was typical of Francis throughout his life. Unfortunately, he later lost the funds that were to be paid him by the sale of the *Union*, so after his second year at the university, at the age of nineteen, he had to leave and was ready to strike out on his own.

With his talents as a printer, he was able to support himself on a variety of newspapers, from the *Burlington* (Iowa) *Hawkeye* to the *New York Tribune*, learning and earning his way as an apprentice printer. It was fine experience for an ambitious young man.

Life In Olympia

In 1871, he turned to the West Coast. He spent the winter in San Francisco and a short time later he was in Steilacoom, a small town in Washington Territory near Olympia, where Catharine's brother Giles was living. Giles Ford died on May 17,

1871, but his widow, Elizabeth, whose first husband, William Affleck, had been in the publishing business, urged Francis to come to Olympia. Francis began his career working as a compositor for the *Puget Sound Courier*. In 1874, he bought the *Olympia Echo* and held the position of editor and publisher. Although he was a Republican, he ran the paper as an independent journal.

The Steilacoom Insane Asylum in 1916, now the Western State Hospital for the Insane, Steilacoom, Washington. *(Public domain photo)*

Before long a situation arose that needed to be brought to the public's attention. Francis Cook had found a cause to publicize, the first of many he was to embrace in his life as a journalist. In this case it was the Steilacoom Insane Asylum, whose operation was desperately in need of changing.

During the early years in Washington Territory, insane persons and those who were mentally deficient were cared for at Vancouver by the Sisters of Charity, the cost being handled on a contractual basis for each individual. This religious group gave good service, but the time came when the governor felt the territory should have its own institution. The site chosen was Fort Steilacoom, from which the troops had been withdrawn in 1868, abandoning the post. The legislature passed an act authorizing the governor and territorial auditor to purchase the buildings from the United States government and turn them over to commissioners who were appointed to look after the care of the insane.

The purchase was made and the buildings improved, all for the betterment of the insane. However, the contract system in use for running the institution proved to be inadequate. A local businessman was given the contract to care for the patients, and a physician was hired to provide medical and psychological care. The business contractor proved to be incompetent, but because he was a political appointee, he could not be replaced. Someone needed to intervene.

The care of these unfortunate people should have been a nonpartisan project—instead it catered to political birds of prey. Francis Cook addressed the problem in the pages of the *Olympia Echo*, even when other papers in Olympia remained silent on the issue, preferring not to antagonize the powerful political influences concerned. With persistent efforts, Francis Cook, together with the Medical Association of Washington, was instrumental in encouraging the 1875 legislature to change the contract, replacing it with a more humane system and one with safeguards against abuse. Without his persistence, it might never have happened.

Francis published the *Echo* for three years, two of the years as a daily. By this time he was ready to move on.

The Move to Tacoma

In April 1877, at the age of twenty-six, Francis Cook moved north of Olympia to New Tacoma. The view southeast from Tacoma was of a magnificent mountain,

Mount Rainier, which may have been an inspiration to Francis in later years when he came to Spokane. He established the *Tacoma Herald*, the first newspaper in the area since the *Tacoma Pacific Tribune* moved to Seattle in 1875. Not long after, Silas and Catharine left their home in Iowa and, with sons Charles and Giles, joined Francis in Washington Territory. They came to Puget Sound from Omaha, reaching Tacoma, the "City of Destiny," in October 1877.

Sometime during this period, Francis built a home in Tacoma. It was a neat-looking, two-story building and must have been a big endeavor for a young man who was establishing a newspaper at the same time. In the 1879 Territorial Census, Francis was living with his parents and his brothers, Charles and Giles.

**Francis Cook's house
in New Tacoma.**

(Photo courtesy Cook family)

6

Mount Rainier, 1910. *(Photo courtesy Paul Dorpat and Jean Sherrard)*

Eventually all of the other Cook sons migrated to Puget Sound, although the oldest, Frederick, remained for only a short time. Several of them were very influential in the area. (Further information about Silas and Catharine Cook and their exceptional sons is discussed in Appendix I.)

Tacoma had been incorporated on November 12, 1875, with a population of less than 500. In 1873, it had been chosen as the western terminus of the Northern Pacific Railroad (the NP). However, the NP had located its depot at New Tacoma, and it was here that Francis began his publication of the *Herald*, a morning daily. It was important to the growing town at the southern end of Puget Sound and was known as the "people's daily."

***Tacoma Herald* Building**
(From the Tacoma Public Library Image Archives)

During his first year of publication, he performed an important journalistic feat. During the 1877 legislative session, Francis went down to Olympia every day, reported the day's work and sent the copy by messenger to Tacoma, part of the trip on horseback, printing this on the same evening. The messenger waited until the paper had been "struck off" and then made his way back, carrying a supply. The report thus distributed reached the people every day seven hours before those of the *Portland Oregonian*, whose work was done by telegraph. It gave Francis Cook considerable prominence in the territory, and it soon helped carry him into the political arena.

New Tacoma was also the headquarters for the Northern Pacific Railway Company. From the beginning of the paper's publication, Francis was critical of the Northern Pacific and its associates, the Oregon State Navigation Company and the Tacoma Land Company. His was the first voice to charge the corporations with taking more from New Tacoma than they gave back. Francis Cook had found a formidable adversary. Never hesitant to face unfavorable odds, Francis Cook took on a giant.

Northern Pacific – The Early Years

The history of the NP is steeped in controversy, which continues to affect our forests today. (For more information, read *Railroads and Clearcuts: Legacy of Congress's 1864 Northern Pacific Railroad Land Grant* by Derrick Jensen and George Draffan.) It began in 1864, during the Civil War, when Abraham Lincoln and the United States Congress *conditionally* granted forty million acres of western America's public domain to build and maintain a railroad from Lake Superior to the Pacific Ocean. Congress retained oversight of this land and the right to *"add to, alter, amend or repeal"* the law, but never, in the ensuing years and with various administrations, has any Congress exercise its right to do this.

The Northern Pacific violated most of the conditions of the law. The NP land grant allowed the acquisition, with conditions, of public lands for the purpose of building and maintaining the railroad. It was granted in alternating square miles, creating a "checkerboard" pattern of ownership, which was intended to increase the value of the acreage that was not granted to the railroad. However, even by the early 1870s, no track had been laid. Such a delay should have voided the grant, but this did not happen.

In 1870, after deadlines had been extended, Congress revised the original grant, enabling the railroad to raise capital by selling bonds. Financier Jay Cooke became directly involved in the sale of Northern Pacific bonds. Much of the money thus earned came from the savings of small farmers, tradesmen and laborers. Another revision of the 1870 grant stipulated that if the Northern Pacific failed financially, it was to sell the remaining grant lands at local auction. In any case, all lands were to be opened to homesteaders within five years of the completion of the railroad. Unfortunately, no lands were legitimately sold at local auctions, and eventually millions of acres of forest land were sold by Northern Pacific to Weyerhaeuser, Potlatch and other timber interests, thus abrogating the original intent of the land grant.

Meanwhile, the Northern Pacific bought out the Chicago, Milwaukee, St. Paul & Pacific Railroad and the control of an Oregon steamboat line. It was well known the management of the Northern Pacific was deficient. Eventually Jay Cooke and the NP collapsed and, in 1875, the railroad was reorganized by Frederick Billings and construction of the railroad lines continued.

The Northern Pacific Fights Back

When the railroad's influence and financial support in the development of the Pacific Northwest was questioned by newspaper editor Francis Cook, the Northern Pacific did not take kindly to the criticism. Cook was urged to run for the legislature in 1878, but the railroad put its power and money behind its own chosen candidates. They waged a vigorous campaign against Cook's run for the legislature in 1878.

During this time the *Tacoma Herald* faced opposition from a newly established paper called the *North Pacific Times*. It was operated by a Mr. and Mrs. Money, former publishers of a paper in Kalama. Their backing in the Tacoma venture came from the Northern Pacific, which leased them the building they used and provided them with all their job printing.

The *Times* and its backers provided Francis with a reason for making a determined fight. In his campaign for the legislature, he alleged coercion, bribery and other forms of corrupt policies against the railroad and the land company. He stood for the people against the corporations. On election day, the "interests" took over many of the polls and worked hard to get votes against Cook. His opponents were involved in several alleged election frauds designed to defeat him, but they failed.

In 1878, Francis Cook was elected to serve on the 1879 Territorial Legislature, representing Pierce, Mason and Chehalis counties. He was elected primarily because of the support of every citizen in Chehalis County. In addition, he had the honor of being chosen presiding officer of the joint session by unanimous vote (the youngest ever to have that honor), in which House Bill #36 was passed creating Spokane County, with the county seat temporarily located at Spokane Falls.

Francis's Trips to Eastern Washington

Before his session in the legislature, Francis made his first trip to Eastern Washington to scout out the topography of the country. He felt certain the Northern Pacific would be extending their lines and he wanted to find for himself the most practical route for the railroad to take. In an interview by Herbert Gaston, printed in the *Chronicle* on June 15, 1914, Cook described this journey as follows:

> I got a pony at The Dalles and with my pack tied on behind the saddle I started my solitary tour of exploration of the Inland Empire. I crossed the Columbia February 8, 1878, and journeyed by way of Goldendale over the Simcoe mountains into and up the Yakima valley, going as far northeast as Ellensburg. Then I turned back, going down the Yakima river to its mouth, then down the Columbia to Wallula, where I crossed on my way to Walla Walla, Dayton and Colfax, and thus up into the Spokane country.

These are the members and the employes of the council or senate of the Washington territorial legislature of 18 , which created Spokane county, separating it from Stevens county. Francis H. Cook, publisher of the first ne per in Spokane, as a member of the council from Pierce, Mason and Chehalis counties. At that time he was p hing newspapers in both New Tacoma and Spokane Falls and claimed residence on the Sound. Mr. Cook, who resident of the council can be seen in the center of the picture. The four men on the left and the four on the ri ith Mr. Cook, constituted the council, the others are the employes. The members of the council are (reading do ft-hand row), James B. LaDu of the lower Columbia counties, G S. Dudley of the lower Sound, G. M. Ringer of W an, R. O. Dunbar of Goldendale, later supreme court justice; (reading up right-hand row) Elliott Cline of W alla, Dr. J. H. Day of Dayton and Amos Tullis of Chehalis.

News clipping of Francis Cook, center, as president, and Washington's territorial legislative body that was responsible for the creation of Spokane County in 1879.

I went on north, generally along the old Mullan road, before I came to Spokane Falls. After examining the country north and then along the old Kentuck Indian trail south to the headwaters of Hangman creek, I made up my mind that the railroad would have to pass through the Spokane valley, and I finally concluded that it would go through by the falls, because of the lay of the land.

At that time people in the east and the directors of the Northern Pacific knew little or nothing of any such place as Spokane or Spokane Falls. The promoters of the road talked of Pend Oreille Lake, Walla Walla and Portland as the spots on the map marking generally the route of the extension after crossing the Rockies.

The topography of the Spokane country looked good to me. I believed it had a bright, but probably a distant future. There was no Riverside avenue then, neither was there a wagon track or trail where that great thoroughfare is now in evidence. But it looked good to me.

The above trip wasn't the only one Francis Cook made into Eastern Washington. Another interesting excursion was described by his wife many years later:

The trip was taken when Indians were numerous and roamed the country at will. With a companion, Mr. Cook left Tacoma on horseback in the summer of 1879 to cross the Cascade mountains. His destination was Spokan Falls. After the start, they heard the Indians were on the warpath. On reaching the summit of the mountains, Mr. Cook and his companion could see the fires of the Indians in the distance. His traveling mate, evidently not caring to meet up with the Indians, slipped out under the cover of darkness and removed a shoe from his horse. The following morning he had a good excuse for not continuing the journey, so Mr. Cook was left to make the journey alone.

However, he did not meet the Indians whose campfires had been seen from the mountain top. In fact, he did not meet any Indians until he reached the place where Moxee City now is located [in Yakima County]. There, to his amazement, he met Chief Smohallah's band of Indian warriors. Too late to evade them, there was nothing to do but show courage. As he approached this band, they, riding two abreast, separated and let Mr. Cook ride through between. He saluted them with "cla-ha-ya, cla-ha-ya," meaning in Chinook, "How do you do?" He received in reply a grunt of disgust.

They were just leaving their camp. An attempt was made to talk Mr. Cook out of his gun, Instead, he evaded the request by pounding his pack pony on the back. The horse seemed much at home among the Indian tepees. Mr. Cook's greatest desire of the moment was to reach the Columbia river and cross to the opposite shore from these warriors. The band was bound for the lower Columbia. There they were to join other Indians for a planned battle. Mr. Cook swam the Columbia river about where Hanford now is located. He continued his way into Spokan Falls without further interference.

Besides his work in the legislature and his new paper in Spokane Falls (*The Spokan Times)*, he found it necessary to expend much of his effort on his Tacoma newspaper. However, after valiantly trying to keep his paper afloat, Francis Cook had to admit the *Herald* could no longer survive. The final issue was published on March 26, 1880.

The *North Pacific Times* had also been forced to cease publication, and New Tacoma was left with no newspaper at all. Cook had been an important voice in the New Tacoma area and was a vigorous fighter for the city's interests. There was never any doubt in his mind that his paper's failure was due to the publication of the *Times* and its promotion by his adversaries: the Northern Pacific Railroad, the Oregon State Navigation Company and the Tacoma Land Company.

In one of its final issues, in January 1880, Francis wrote the following:

> The management of the OSN, NPRR and the Tacoma land companies—with great promises and bright expectations—infused the first filthy breath of life into the disreputable sheet which has succumbed to its own rottenness.

Ceasing publication of the *Herald* must have been a difficult decision for Francis Cook, but he was far too resilient to allow it to keep him down for long. He had some other plans brewing in the back of his mind. His time spent in Spokane Falls had convinced him his future lay in Eastern Washington. His thoughts were seriously turning to the new town rising on the banks of the Spokane River. During Francis's visits to Spokane, he met some of the more important citizens there at the time. He was convinced this Eastern Washington town had the possibilities of becoming an important factor in Washington Territory and would need a newspaper. Early in 1879, he made arrangements for moving to Spokane and found a place to send his presses and equipment.

While he was seriously planning this move, something far more important was occupying his time and his thoughts. On one of his trips through Pierce County, he had met and fallen in love with the woman who was to become his wife—Laura Candace McCarty, who was living with her parents in Sumner, Washington.

Laura McCarty, the young woman Francis Cook chose to be his life's partner, was a person of excellent character and background, and a woman of intelligence and education. She was to be his helpmate, both at home and in business, and the mother of their eleven children.

Laura McCarty and Francis Cook

On June 24, 1880, Francis Cook and Laura Candace McCarty were married at her home in Sumner. It was a most fortuitous decision for Francis Cook. In the years to come, Laura proved to be a wonderful wife, mother and helpmate, and one who was adored by her children. She was certainly an intelligent and articulate woman as evidenced by the many excellent articles she wrote in later years.

The newly wedded couple was prepared to meet the challenges of living in a small but growing town in Eastern Washington, leaving their dearly loved families behind. They were on a journey that would result in making important contributions to Spokane, Washington.

Laura Candace McCarty **Francis Henry Cook**

Married June 24, 1880, in Sumner, Washington
(Photos courtesy Cook family)

The Francis H. Cook monument in Riverside Memorial Park (cemetery) was dedicated on October 26, 2007. Cook was the president of the Washington Territorial Legislative Council that created Spokane County in 1879. He became one of Spokane's early pioneers and was responsible, among other accomplishment, for the first newspaper and first motorized trolley in Spokane. His many other endeavors are covered within this study. Family members attending the memorial ceremony, shown from left, are: Nancy Swanson, Kathleen Cook, Laura Poulin, Lori Ashe, Marcia Harken, David Fray, Gwen Yoke and Charles Yoke. *(Photo courtesy Tony and Suzanne Bamonte)*

Section II
The Cook Family In Spokane

Francis and Laura's Arrival in Spokane

During 1879, Francis took his printing and job presses and other equipment to Spokane Falls, going via the Columbia River to Almota, then north to Spokane, but thanks to severe weather conditions, the shipment was held up in Colfax and could move no further. It was temporarily housed in the offices of the *Palouse Gazette*. Publication was not to be halted, however, and the first two issues of the *Spokan Times* were printed in Colfax and delivered to Spokane Falls by horseback. Francis's brother Charles later wrote he had run off the first issues, so he apparently had accompanied his brother on the trip.

It should be noted Francis Cook always spelled the name of the town "Spokan," without the letter "e" at the end, as he felt it was phonetically correct. Thus the name of his new paper was the *Spokan Times*. In the first issue, dated April 24, 1879, Francis wrote and published an essay about all of Washington Territory, from Puget Sound and the Cascades to Eastern Washington, and described the area around Spokane in glowing terms. The following is a brief excerpt:

> **Northeastern Washington**. There is probably no country now known to the American people, the name of which sounds so pleasantly upon the ear of the homeless and unsettled as that of Northeastern Washington. Only distance from the more densely populated countries prevents Eastern Washington from becoming, in a single season, a very populous region. For years and years after the discovery of this great country, the green grass waved over an almost pathless meadow; the waters of the Spokan thundered through an uninhabited region; and nature, clothed in the habiliments of promised wealth and surpassing grandeur, remained unadorned and unappropriated. But, as the restless wave of immigration pressed its way across the American Plains; swept over the Rocky Mountains; and finally, rested upon the Pacific's peaceful shore, the curiosity of the most curious brought a very few families into the country now known as Northeastern Washington. [For a complete transcription of the essay, see Appendix III.]

As soon as weather permitted, the *Spokan Times* moved to Spokane. It was housed in a small wooden building on Front Street, between Post and Mill (now Wall) streets, where Francis lived until he returned to New Tacoma for his marriage. The deed to the property was recorded on July 15, 1880, showing James Glover, J. J. Browne and A. M. Cannon and wives as grantors and Francis Cook and Laura as grantees. Purchase amount was $1.00.

On July 4, 1879, the *Spokan Times* published its first "special edition," describing the festivities to be held that day to celebrate the signing of the Declaration of Independence. Francis proudly described the rapid growth of Spokan Falls:

> We now number 35 families, two general merchandise stores, two hotels, one restaurant, one meat market, one flouring and one saw mill, one jewelry store, one blacksmith shop, two livery stables, one carpenter shop, one brewery, three saloons, one newspaper, and still they are coming!

He went on to describe the activities of the day—the opening ceremony and the parade going through the downtown area, ending at College Grove (about where Lewis & Clark High School now stands). There was to be music by a band and the Spokan Falls glee club, a prayer, the reading of the Declaration of Independence, an oration, and the singing of the "Star-Spangled Banner," followed by dinner with lunch baskets.

> After these, those interested in the national game of baseball can repair to the grounds near the grove and witness the game; at the close of which the procession will re-form and march back to town. In the evening, a grand ball will be given in the new hall of Cornelius & Davis. All are invited to attend.

Francis then revealed his somewhat Puritanical opinion of the ball:

> One important lesson is always taught by our Fourth of July festivities, but is seldom or never heeded by those who learn it by bitter experience. The lesson is this: the dance which follows the celebration is generally demoralizing in its nature. While it may be a source of pleasure to the participants, it encroaches upon their time, robs them of sleep and cripples their best energies for succeeding days. When people will hang around the ballroom all night long, engaging in the enlivening dance, eating a hearty supper of cakes and pies and exposing themselves to the best agents of colds and dyspepsia, it is positive evidence the foot-killer has not been attending to his business as closely as he should.

The 1880 U.S. Census for Spokane Falls, which was taken on June 24-26, includes Francis Cook, age twenty-eight, "Editor of the Spokan Times." Although this establishes Cook's residency in Spokane Falls at that time, he could not have been physically present when the census was taken, as he was in Sumner being married on the 24th. However, the next entry on the page is that of a 23-year-old printer by the name of White, who was probably Francis's assistant. Besides listing himself, White must have given the name of Francis Cook to the census enumerator. Of special note, he gave Francis's birthplace as Ohio, but did not give a birthplace for either of the Cook parents. If Francis had been there on the 24th to speak to the census taker, he would have been able to furnish his parents' birthplaces.

Years later, in 1933, Laura wrote several articles for the *Spokane Chronicle*. By that time, Francis had long been dead, and Laura was living in Yakima with her daughter, Katharine Cook Alvis. One of the articles described their wedding trip and their arrival at Spokane Falls:

> After a wedding breakfast, I bade goodbye to father, mother, sister and brothers and the home of my childhood, to go to a new and comparatively unknown country. That afternoon

we went to Tacoma and took the train next morning for Kalama. From there, we went by steamer to Portland, where we remained for two days. We then started again for Spokan Falls. We traveled by boat up the mighty Columbia, with its marvelous scenery, to The Dalles, and then by train for a short distance, made necessary by the rapids. It was there the locks later were constructed. Next we took a steamer to the mouth of the Snake river, just below Pasco. There we entered the Snake river and continued by boat for about 90 miles to Almota, then by stage to Spokan Falls.

It was a long and arduous trip for Francis and his new bride. However, his enthusiasm for Spokane Falls was seconded by his bride, when she and Francis arrived at their new home after their wedding trip. In Laura's words:

> We reached Spokan Falls July 3, 1880. I was delighted with the place from the first. As we entered it that summer evening from Hangman creek, the gravelly plain covered with tall bunch grass and surrounded by evergreen pines on the south, the river on the north with its several falls rushing and foaming through in a hurry to join the mighty Columbia, the grand, snow-capped mountains to the northeast, made an enchanting scene, never to be forgotten. It was indeed in restful contrast to the tedious stage coach ride across the dusty country between the Snake river and Spokan Falls.

Laura Cook was enthusiastic about her new home, and she was ready for the challenges to come in the young western town. Many years later, she was to say of those early days:

> Our first weeks in Spokan were spent at the home of Rev. Mr. and Mrs. H. T. Cowley. Mr. Cook had purchased an acre from Mr. Cowley and had begun our first home, but it was not ready for us to move in until later. Also our household goods were delayed in arriving on account of the Columbia River being high.

The Cooks' purchase of an acre of land from Rev. Cowley is found nowhere in Spokane land records. It was probably an unrecorded transaction, as it seems unlikely Laura would have made that statement if it were not true.

The Location of the *Spokan Times*

Questions arise as to where the *Spokan Times* was located in the tiny town of Spokane Falls. Originally on Front Street, its permanent home was at the southeast corner of Howard and Riverside. However, there are several conflicting accounts about the details.

1) James Glover claimed he gave the land to Francis Cook. Glover wrote his *Reminiscences*, first printed in the *Spokane Chronicle* in 1917 and later published as a book of that title. Here he stated: "I gave him one of the finest lots in town in consideration of locating here. It was 60-feet wide and extended clear through from Riverside to Sprague on the east side of Howard street."

2) Francis Cook claimed the gift must have slipped Glover's mind, because he had paid $50.00 for the property.

3) Laura Cook, in later years, stated, "Francis had arranged with J. N. Glover to advertise Spokan Falls in the *Tacoma Herald* in return for half a lot on the southeast corner of Howard and Riverside."

Actually, Spokane County land records show all three of these accounts contain elements of truth. Land records in early American and early western development are, at best, a vital but sometimes questionable source for researchers and should be approached with caution. What appears to be the truth is sometimes not. Patricia Law Hatcher, one of the foremost authorities on United States land records, includes the following pertinent remarks in her book *Locating Your Roots*:

> Early in America's history, there was no requirement that deeds be recorded, although a recorded deed might be considered more binding or to have precedence over an unrecorded deed. Eventually laws were passed requiring deeds to be recorded, in part to help the county in tax collection. Needless to say, there was no great rush to comply. You will find in some localities almost all deeds were promptly recorded, but in other localities (or other time periods), the opposite may be true. ... We often find deeds recorded years, even decades, later, when the land was finally sold out of the family.

> When reading deeds, it is always wise to look forward and backward through the deed books to see if related deeds were filed at the same time. There may be an unrelated deed or two recorded in between. Some clerks seem to have put loose deeds into a stack to be copied into the book later, not always in the expected order.

On researching the three reports, the following notes provide some answers:

1) Assuming these people were telling the truth as they saw it, Laura's statement will be considered first, as she had nothing to gain or lose by lying and was undoubtedly telling it as she remembered. The key to her statement was the "trade" Glover made by giving "half a lot" to Cook in exchange for advertising in the *Tacoma Herald*. That could only have happened before March 1880, as Cook had no connection with the *Herald* after that time. It is a fact Francis advertised Spokane Falls in the *Herald* while he still owned the paper, a fact that is verified by reading copies of the newspaper. A trade of land for advertising could easily have occurred on one of Cook's early visits to Spokane Falls and would have been a good deal for Francis, because Glover had a major financial stake in selling property at the falls.

2) It does appear Glover, Cannon and Browne gave Cook the property on Front Street known as "Lot 3, Block 12," the first home of the *Spokan Times*. It was purchased for $1.00, so was virtually a gift as Glover stated.

3) James Glover, whose business dealings were sometimes questionable and was later an opponent of Cook's, might have had reason to lie about his generosity in giving Cook the property. However, it is possible Mr. Glover's memory of this event nearly forty years later was faulty. He did give Cook one-half of the lot at Howard and Riverside as a trade. His statement that the lot extended "clear through from Riverside to Sprague" is incorrect, as he gave Cook only one-half of that lot.

4) Francis was only partially correct when he claimed he paid $50.00 for the property, as his purchase of Lot 5, Block 20 from Glover, Browne and Cannon for that amount was for the remaining half of the lot. This was the property on the southeast corner of Howard and Riverside, where Francis erected a two-story building. The deed was not recorded until July 26, 1883, but Cook purchased the land much earlier. Laura later stated: "Before the arrival of the Northern Pacific railway in 1881, Mr. Cook had erected a two-story frame building on his lot at Riverside and Howard."

The first floor of the Cooks' two-story building was occupied by the NPRR in 1881, and the printing office with its signal station was on the second floor, where Francis and Laura also made their home for several years. Apparently Francis's earlier disagreements with the NP were now a thing of the past. This building was eventually torn down and replaced by the Spokane National Bank, which was destroyed in the 1889 fire. It was replaced by the Rookery Building, which was torn down and replaced in the early 2000s by a parking lot.

During the early years, Laura spent most of her time in the print shop helping out. She became adept at setting type and handling distribution and doing other necessary work, although she later said she never wrote any of the editorials. She enjoyed the challenge, and it kept her busy until the babies began to arrive. In all her reminiscences, she was a cheerleader for her husband. In her eyes, he was always a champion of the people.

Francis Cook and the *Spokan Times*

Ralph Dyar's authorized history of the *Spokesman-Review* newspaper, *News For An Empire*, describes Spokane's first editor, Francis H. Cook, as a "tramp printer." This is not accurate. Francis had indeed been an apprentice printer in his younger days, when he went from town to town working as a typesetter and pressman. However, by the time he came to Spokane, he had been an owner, publisher and editor of an Iowa and two coastal newspapers, and had been the president of the territorial legislature— hardly what one would call a tramp printer, an inappropriate and somewhat insulting choice of words. He accomplished a dream by furnishing the town of Spokane with its first newspaper.

The townspeople were pleased with the advent of their first newspaper, but a new voice in an already established area sometimes is not welcome to everyone. Francis Cook was never hesitant about speaking his mind and never worried about the consequences. When he saw something he felt was wrong or was not in the general interest of the public, he wrote about it and, of course, suffered the consequences.

The *Northwest Tribune* of Cheney, sometimes a critic of Spokane activities, was complimentary of Spokane Falls in its November 12, 1880, issue: "Last week we made a visit to the prosperous town (Spokane) which has now attained a considerable prominence all over the Pacific coast." The article mentions many well-known families of Spokane at that time, whose names remained prominent well into the 20th century: James N. Glover, F. R. Moore, and A. M. Cannon, as well as businessmen Frederick Berg, J. S. Graham, and Louis Zeigler, among others.

It described Spokane as a pretty place and, with keen foresight, declared: "Some day a first class educational institution will be established here and no place will enjoy more religious advantages." The November 12th edition also included a column from nearby Deep Creek—written on October 27th, author unknown—which was not complimentary to Francis Cook. There is no explanation for the following harsh words:

> We consider Francis Cook, publisher of the *Spokan Times*, to be too poor a specimen of the editorial fraternity to waste many words on, so we will drop him here.

A month later the *Tribune* criticized Cook because he was trying to recruit new businesses to Spokane Falls, when representatives of those businesses already existed in the town. Apparently the *Tribune* felt competitive business should not be given the opportunity to advertise.

> While it is properly right for any newspaper man to solicit business for his paper ... the course of the *Times* editor is denounced by the entire newspaper fraternity as dishonorable, unprofessional and productive of the rebuke he is now receiving—the strong condemnation of all businessmen.

Francis Cook was able to take this sort of criticism in stride, and by June of 1881 announced that, after July 1st, his paper would be published six days a week. He remarked on June 30th: "Already the citizens interested in the growth of this new country have guaranteed a liberal support for the *Daily Times*, which will enable us to print a creditable little paper. It is very pleasant to notice the marked interest taken in this enterprise by every business man and friend of progress."

Competition from the Chronicle

Not every businessman agreed. Three of the "prominent" town fathers in Spokane Falls were eager to join the critics. In opposition to Cook's paper, on June 29, 1881, James Glover, along with assistance from good friends, A. M. Cannon and J. J. Browne, started a newspaper of their own, the *Spokane Chronicle*. Its editor was a man by the name of C. B. Carlisle, about whom very little is known.

Unfortunately, the first issues of the *Chronicle* no longer exist, but early editorials that are available were critical of both Francis Cook and the *Spokan Times*. James Glover, owner of the *Chronicle*, couldn't resist writing his own opinion. His words were insulting and, in some instances, untrue. In the issue of September 28, 1881, Glover wrote:

> As the fellow, Cook, who runs the advertising sheet here, misnamed a newspaper, has seen fit to attack me personally, forbearance has ceased to be a virtue. ... this fellow Cook has been a detriment to this people. The paper has been the laughing stock of the community and principally noted for the callow ignorance exhibited and the unusual shelling of the truth. Just after starting here, he explained he needed money to pay freight on his press ... to pay it back in thirty days. I loaned him $100. He sneaked away and to this day, I hold that due bill. ... I should have compelled him to pay it long ago but for the sake of his wife who is a lady. [He proceeded to belabor Cook for his treatment of the boys who worked for him, and finished with the following]: Cook is, too, a pillar of the Congregational Church – a Trustee. He subscribed $50 which is yet to be paid. And this is the fellow that whines for the support of this people ... (signed) J. N. Glover.

Cook, not willing to be the recipient of such insults, rose to the occasion and came back on October 4, 1881, with the following:

> The effort of J. N. Glover to blackmail the editor of this paper in the last issue of his organ [the *Chronicle*], and his threats to continue in the same line, may possibly bring him a better [bitter?] harvest than the most sanguine of his class can even expect before he has finished the job he has undertaken of wiping *The Times* out of existence. So far, he has merited and received the scorn and derision of all good citizens for his blackmailing scheme. They know very well that his object is to prevent us from discussing questions which he wants to take advantage of the public. While they believe him to be willing to undertake a blackmailing scheme, they question his discretion in this instance. Were it of a private nature, the public would not take so much interest in the matter. But they see an effort put forth to prevent an independent and free newspaper from protecting the interests of the people under all circumstances. He does this simply because his interests and those of his little band are not in common with the public's best interests.

Aside from the spiteful bickering between these two men, it appears that Glover may have made an error in mentioning the missing subscription to the Congregational Church in the September 28th issue. Westminster Congregational Church was founded in 1879 and, among the ten founders, the name of Francis Cook does not appear. However, in June 1883, Francis and Laura were both among the founders of the First Presbyterian Church and remained members for the rest of their lives. Laura's parents had founded the First Presbyterian Church in Sumner, Washington, and it seems a natural conclusion that Francis and Laura both preferred the Presbyterian Church. There is no evidence James Glover was ever a member of any of the churches in Spokane, and one has to wonder how he found out about the alleged "$50 outstanding subscription."

Spokane's First Presbyterian Church, of which Francis and Laura Cook were charter members, was built near the corner of Riverside and Monroe in 1886. The little building on the corner in front of the church housed the early *Review.* *(Photo from* Spokane and the Inland Empire *by N. W. Durham, 1912)*

These two sketches are of the first and second First Presbyterian Church buildings. The one on the left, dedicated on December 15, 1886, is the church shown in the top photo. The second building, in use until June 1910, was located at the corner of Second and Jefferson. Laura Cook was the last surviving charter member of this church.
(Sketches from First Presbyterian Church, 45th anniversary booklet published in 1928)

JAMES N. and SUSAN CRUMP GLOVER

Known as the "Father of Spokane," James N. Glover has enjoyed a good reputation, much of it well deserved. He certainly foresaw the possibilities in the tiny settlement he found at the falls on the Spokane River in early 1873, at which time he purchased the acreage that would eventually be the town site of Spokane Falls. His enthusiasm was boundless. As he said many years later in his *Reminiscences of James N. Glover*: "I liked the beautiful, clear stream of water. I liked the falls, with their foundation of basaltic rock that would remain forever. The whole situation aroused my desire of possession. I never have been able to express the force with which this country impressed my mind at the time I first saw it. ... I refused to leave, because I saw that someday my expectations must be realized."

James N. Glover
(Photo from Spokane Falls and Its Exposition, *1890)*

To anyone who loves the city of Spokane and the area surrounding it, Glover's determination and dedication are to be admired. He foresaw the possibilities in the area and invested his thoughts, time and money to make it a reality. In this regard, he deserves our respect and gratitude.

However, with further study, one finds a less-flattering side to James Glover. He was a man who could not and would not tolerate opposition. With him, there were never two sides to an issue. There was only one side—his. Unfortunately, this man, who possessed an intelligent mind, could not accept the fact that someone else might also have an opinion worth considering. It kept Glover from being a truly exceptional city father.

He also was not a very good husband. He married Susan Crump in Salem, Oregon, in 1868. She was an attractive young lady of twenty-five, and presumably the couple was deeply in love. In 1873, he accompanied her on her first trip to the falls, leaving her family and friends behind to come to a strange and lonely place. From the very first, her husband was continually occupied in the building and development of the new town. Although they made friends among the first settlers, Susan was often left alone to cope with life as best she could. Her loneliness led to periods of deep melancholia (or depression), which her husband either failed to recognize or ignored and neglected to find the necessary help for her. Eventually her mental health was destroyed.

Her story is a tragic one, perhaps the saddest of which is that she is rarely noted anywhere. In his *Reminiscences,* in which Glover described his life in Spokane in great detail, Susan's name is never mentioned. The only picture of

Susan Crump Glover, c. 1882.
(Photo from the Barbara Cochran collection, courtesy Tony and Suzanne Bamonte)

Glover's wife in the book is that of Esther Leslie, the woman he married soon after he divorced Susan and had her committed to Eastern State Hospital, a mental asylum at Medical Lake, in 1899, where she remained until her death on October 11, 1921. (For a detailed study of the life of Susan Crump Glover, anyone interested is urged to read *Seven Frontier Women and the Founding of Spokane Falls,* written by Barbara Cochran, edited by Suzanne and Tony Bamonte.)

This is a brief description of a man who refused to accept Francis H. Cook as a deserving adversary, but considered him someone who should be ruined. It is not a particularly flattering portrait of the "Father of Spokane."

Deepening Controversy

The *Northwest Tribune,* on October 11, 1881, was exceedingly pro-Cook in the matter and was not hesitant to publish its thoughts on the subject:

> When town proprietors and bosses conceive the idea of squelching their local paper, it is pretty good evidence that there is something buried which they, the town proprietors, do not want exhumed. We predict that such is the case with J. N. Glover, who has undertaken to snuff out the *Spokan Times.* ... The people are generally correct in their verdict on such schemes, and so far as we have heard they approve of the course of the *Times,* while they frown down the contemptible action of the "bosses." A newspaper must represent the masses, not the interest of a few town proprietors. If Glover has money enough to play his organ, no one objects to it so long as the public are not compelled to listen. Carlisle, who is playing second for Glover's organ at the Falls, is proving himself not only a ninny, but a disrespecter of the truth.

October 18th brought a lengthy editorial from the *Times,* describing the various projects the paper had endorsed since its inception, such as creating a new county out of Stevens County, attempting to locate the county seat at Spokane, and spanning the Spokane River with a free bridge. According to Cook, all of these endeavors had been opposed by "the ring." The *Times* described this in detail:

> In order to have an organ of their own with which to mislead the public whenever occasion might offer an opportunity, the ring decided to purchase press and type, and to select some-

one who would do just what they wanted him to do—no matter how low they might wish him to stoop. They had to do this, for no honest man can represent the true interests of this city and county, and at the same time serve the ring. The interests of the ring are not identical with those of our citizens. ... They foster no enterprise but such as pays them tribute.

Meanwhile the Cooks' personal life had changed considerably. While Francis was conducting his exposure of "the Bosses" (or "the Ring," as he often called them), Laura gave birth to their first child, Katharine Ruth, born November 11, 1881, named after her two grandmothers, Catharine Cook and Ruth McCarty. The little family was still living upstairs in the *Spokan Times* building. Laura helped with the publication of the newspaper when she wasn't busy with the baby, so she was well aware of the negative feelings between her husband and some of the important Spokane businessmen.

In the *Times* issue of February 25, 1882, Francis Cook unleashed his vitriolic pen in an editorial against *Chronicle* editor Carlisle, a portion of which follows:

It is very seldom that any person, no matter how degraded, renders himself so completely obnoxious in as short a time as has the man Carlisle, who for the present edits the *Spokan* [*sic*] *Falls Chronicle*. ... He is the most conceited and cowardly hypocritical scoundrel that has ever disgraced our community. By nature he is a constitutional liar and coward. ... Since the very first he has done all in his power to injure those who would not cooperate with him in his useless tirade against his competitors. But he has been careful to do it in a cowardly way that would keep that pretty countenance from harm. Well, this —no, I will not say this man—for he is not a man; he, Carlisle, is a miscarriage and a monstrosity at that—a monstrosity of a liar and blackmailer. ... The writer of this article is personally responsible for what he says here, and if the fellow referred to takes exceptions, he may have his satisfaction.

Cook wasn't finished with Carlisle yet, however. On March 4th he had more to say about the "acknowledged crank and liar of the *Chronicle*." He described many occasions when Carlisle had misrepresented or lied about something. Cook claimed Carlisle had "forced himself" upon the city council as a clerk and, in reading and publishing public documents, introduced words that were not supposed to be there, and went among the public deliberately intending to mislead honest people by falsehoods and misrepresentations. Cook ended by saying: "He is abhorred by decent people, and is despised by those who claim to be his friends on account of the possible good his services may be to them."

Later in March, shortly before the city election was due, the *Times* published the following opinion:

One of the Bosses wants to be mayor and that ought to create an interest. Four more want to be re-elected as Sub-bosses to A. M'Cannon (we here give the name as it used to be). The people plainly see that such a result would jeopardize the interests of our city. It is a foregone conclusion that most of the Bosses in this city must soon bid farewell to official pap, and see official positions they themselves have occupied so unacceptably to the people during the past. It is too well understood to admit of contradiction that a majority of the present city council can be advantageously spared; that is, laid on the shelf, or bottled, to improve with age.

The "Boss," of course, was James Glover. Actually, Cannon's full name was Anthony McHugh (or McCue) Cannon. Cannon definitely considered Cook's spelling of his name to be an insult. It added to the huge troubles to come between the two men. Another *Times* editorial advised that the present council should not be trusted due to the fact that "Cannon's paper and his notorious tool and liar [Carlisle] recommend their reelection."

The Assault in Cook's Office

By the end of March, the situation between Cook and his adversaries in the city came to a climax. Francis and his paper had alienated several of the more important individuals in Spokane Falls, some of whom were anxious for retribution. Strangely enough, his fight did not involve Carlisle, who might have had justification because of the libelous statements printed against him. Instead, the confrontation came from A. M. Cannon, who really didn't like it that Cook had used an incorrect spelling of his name.

In addition, Cook printed allegations that Cannon had been illegally cutting timber on government lands. While Cannon settled the matter with the government by paying for the timber, Francis was not complimentary to Cannon in writing about the incident.

All the details of what happened on March 31, 1882, are not known today, because the surviving accounts are conflicting. The following description, which was printed in the *Spokan Times*, April 1, 1882, is taken from Francis Cook's version of the event:

MURDEROUS ASSAULT

A. M. Cannon and B. H. Bennett [his son-in-law] of the bank in this city, called at the residence of Francis H. Cook last evening, and finding he had not returned from town, wanted to know where he was, saying they might meet him. The visit was occasioned by articles published in the *Times* to which Mr. Cannon took exception. At ten o'clock today Cannon and Bennett entered the *Times* office on the second floor, while none were present but Mr. and Mrs. Cook with a babe in the cradle. Cannon demanded retraction, and swore Mr. Cook must sign papers [not then shown] or he would kill him. The editor did not do so, and Cannon drew a revolver to carry out his threat.

Mr. Cook took up an iron side-stick (used in the office) and induced Cannon to put away his revolver; whereupon Bennett drew a revolver, stating that he was going to take part in the affair, even while Mrs. Cook pleaded with him to desist. As Bennett was trying to shoot, Cook took up another iron and knocked the weapon out of his hand. Cannon's aim was again being taken, with Mrs. Cook in line, when Mr. Cook knocked the revolver out of his hand and across the room. Bennett, by this time, had regained his weapon, but his left hand was stricken down by Mr. Cook. Cannon, who had regained his deadly weapon on the opposite side of the room, raised it to fire; but Mr. Cook threw a missile that hit him just as he was pulling the trigger, the weapon discharging and the bullet passing through the stovepipe, glancing to the ceiling.

After this the blows fell rapidly, blood was scattered over the room, a case of type was pied [mixed up], and the men closed in close embrace. Mrs. Cook had rushed downstairs, and a crowd began to gather. By this time Mr. Cook had regained his feet, and the assaulting party had ceased their efforts. After regaining the street, and after Mr. Cook had given up his piece of printing material, Cannon again threatened to kill Mr. Cook, but bystanders interfered. Warrants for the arrest of Cannon and Bennett have been issued, but neither will be able to be out, perhaps, for weeks. Both are under the care of physicians, and the scalp wounds they received, which are very severe, have been sewed up. Mr. Cook was not injured, but was somewhat tired.

From the *Northwest Tribune* of Friday, March 31, 1882:

THE SPOKANE FALLS TRAGEDY

The public is generally familiar with the personal feelings existing between the editor of the Spokane *Times* and some of the leading citizens of that city. For several weeks the *Times* has waged a warfare against several of the townsmen, and on Wednesday proceedings culminated in the tragic manner in which several lives were endangered, if not lost. These particulars ... were about as follows:

A few days ago a government official arrived in the Falls to examine and settle with different parties who had been cutting timber on the government lands. Among his number was A. M. Cannon, a gentleman largely interested in the Falls and proprietor of the saw mill. Mr. Cannon and the government official at once settled matters satisfactorily by paying the government price for the timber. The *Daily Times* in alluding to the matter the next day referred to Mr. Cannon in terms anything but complimentary, whereupon Mr. Cannon, accompanied by his bank cashier, Mr. Bennett, proceeded to the office of the *Times* and demanded a retraction, which was refused.

What was said first or who fired the first shot, we have been unable to learn, but a shot from some revolver was followed by a bitter contest in which Messrs. Cannon and Bennett sustained serious though not dangerous injuries....

It is an unfortunate circumstance for our sister city and will be generally regretted. As the matter will probably go into the courts we will refrain from any opinion tending to bias the public mind.

On April 14, 1882, the *Northwest Tribune* published the version of the Cook/Cannon affair as written in the *Chronicle*, saying, "it seems to be a very fair statement." Portions differing from the story as it appeared in the *Times* follow:

The morning of the affray, A. M. Cannon, although still smarting under the injury done him, fully decided to have no quarrel with Cook, but to take a witness, B. H. Bennett, go to the office of the *Times*, show Cook wherein he was wrong and ask him to retract his statements. ... "I was looking for you last night, and it is probably a good thing that I didn't find you, as I was angry." ... Cook wanted to know the first objection, and Mr. Cannon asked him for his authority for saying that his name was McCannon. Cook said: "old Masonic records." Mr. Cannon said Cook knew that was false, as neither had any access to such records; that Cook would have no trouble to learn all about him [Mr. Cannon].

At this Cook partly rose, in a threatening attitude, with a "side-stick" in each hand, until then lying beside him on the desk, when Bennett drew his revolver and told Cook to lay down the weapons and they would talk the matter out. Cook laid them down, or partly so, when Mr. Bennett put his pistol in his pocket, as did Mr. Cannon. [Please note: nothing had been said up to this point that Mr. Cannon even had a revolver.]

At that instant, Cook snatched both side sticks and struck both Mr. Cannon and Mr. Bennett. He struck Mr. Bennett twice and Mr. Cannon two or three times, when the latter, seeing that Cook intended to kill him, if possible, drew his pistol and shot at, but missed him. He then closed in upon Cook, and forced him to the floor, struggling for the possession of the "side-stick." Cook finally begged Mr. Cannon not to kill him for his wife's sake, and said he would retract all he had ever said about Mr. Cannon in the paper. Mr. Cannon let up on him at the door when Cook rushed out of the office and into the street. With the "side-stick" Cook inflicted a number of wounds upon both gentlemen, but after a day of rest at home both resumed their business as usual.

In the same article, the following quote from the *Portland* (Oregon) *Standard* was included:

The account as published was telegraphed by Cook and gave his side of the story which is by no means a truthful version of the affair. ... Neither Bennett nor Cannon were injured so as to prevent them from attending to their business next day. The public sentiment is strongly in favor of Cannon and Bennett, and condemns the course pursued by Cook in his personal abuse of the leading citizens of Spokane. Cook is not known to leave many friends at any place he has lived and he has about played himself out in his present residence. Messrs. Cannon and Bennett are, on the other hand, highly respected and we may say as much of all the others that Cook has been venting his malice upon. [The question arises as to why the Portland newspaper became involved in the Cook/Cannon affair. However, both Cannon and Glover had earlier lived in the Oregon city.]

The grand jurors for the April term of court, due to meet in Cheney on the 10th of April, had been chosen by the 1st of April. The leading juror was James N. Glover. Cannon and Bennett, who had been bound over to appear before the grand jury on a charge of attempt to commit murder, were not indicted. The matter was then closed. Francis Cook wrote his last opinion on the subject, publishing an article in the *Times* on April 22nd:

A GRAND FARCE

The fact A. M. Cannon and B. H. Bennett were not indicted was not owing to a lack of all the evidence necessary under ordinary circumstances. In older settlements, where law is properly respected and rigidly enforced, such a crime as they committed would have been punished by imprisonment in the penitentiary for a fixed number of years. The names of witnesses placed in the hands of the proper authorities, could truthfully testify Cannon stated before he made the attack, when remonstrated with, that he "had the law in his pocket," and that Cannon and Bennett left the bank when they expected and probably knew no one was to be present in the office but their intended victim and his wife and child. They turned out of their natural course, to avoid notice, passed down over a gulch, crossed the ravine, came behind and between buildings to a point on Howard street, where they quickly crossed over and entered the office.

Anthony M. Cannon
(Photo from Spokane Falls and Its Exposition, *1890)*

Entering in a friendly manner, they chose their positions and after a few words Cannon stated in a loud voice that he "feared neither God, man nor the devil," and he "would kill" the editor if he did not do as he wished him to do; Bennett saying, as he also drew a revolver, "I am going to take a part in this." Each attempted twice to shoot Mr. Cook, but were prevented from so doing by having their arms struck down by an iron "side-stick." The man whose life they were vainly struggling to end in the presence of his wife and babe, had it in his power to kill them, and gave them sufficient punishment for their attempt to murder.

They have evidence of these facts on their persons to-day. After this encounter was ended, and Mr. Cook had given up his iron bar, Cannon again attacked him on the street with words too vile to print, cocked his revolver and threatened to shoot Mr. Cook. This was witnessed by over twenty of our citizens. He acknowledged having shot at Mr. Cook while in the office, and wondered why he did not hit him.

Bascomb H. Bennett
(Photo from Spokane Falls Illustrated, *1889)*

The above statements are facts, and can be clearly PROVEN by the witnesses whose names were given the prosecuting attorney for this district. That Cannon and Bennett were not indicted is no evidence that they were not guilty, because the above facts are well understood by the residents of this city, and are commented upon by people all over the Northwest. We are almost ashamed to tell the world that such an atrocious crime goes unpunished, but such is the history of all new countries. Until this country is more densely settled, and its inhabitants respect the law, we must respect the law, we must expect the rich and vicious to escape just punishment, while the poor are given no quarter whatever.

So ended the grievous affair that justifiably created a sensation throughout Spokane and the Northwest. It proved to be the end of Francis Cook's involvement in journalism, as he was understandably disenchanted with the whole business. Within three weeks after the above article was written, the *Northwest Tribune* announced the following in its issue of May 12, 1882:

Both newspapers at Spokane Falls have changed hands. Mr. D. T. Herron having purchased the *Times*, will change its name to *Independent*, and H. E. Allen & Co. are the new proprietors of the *Chronicle*. We extend the fraternal hand to our new neighbors while regretting to sever our pleasant relations with the former managers of both papers.

Francis Cook had lost his fight, but he had not lost his faith. A man who was always looking ahead to new horizons, he was ready and able to change his life and find new challenges.

Francis Cook, Farmer and Entrepreneur

Francis Cook was not a man to look back. Editing and publishing a newspaper had been his primary reason for coming to Spokane. It was a business he enjoyed, but now it was gone and there is no evidence he ever thought about the printing business again. That phase of his life was over, and he was able to accept it and move on. Many years later, his fourth child Clara said, "Others didn't seem to have the ability to go ahead like Father did. He had so many irons in the fire." Clara was right. There was always a new project on Francis Cook's horizon.

Beginning in February 1884, Francis Cook's following significant land purchases in Spokane were filed, all of them in Township 25:

- February 9, 1884: Warranty Deed from NPRR; NW¼ of Section 29
  – 160 acres
- February 19, 1884: Warranty Deed from NPRR; NW¼ of Section 32
  – 160 acres
- May 20, 1884: United States Patent; SW¼ of SW¼ of SW¼ of Section 20
  – 40 acres
- November 1, 1886: Warranty Deed from NPRR; SW¼ of Section 29
  – 160 acres
- February 9, 1886: Certificate of Sale from NPRR; SE¼ of Section 29
  – 160 acres

Thus, within a few short years, Cook was in possession of 680 acres of choice property on the heights south of the city. The forty-acre property was the nearest to town—just one mile from downtown Spokane. A portion of the acreage was platted as Cook's 1st, 2nd, 3rd and 4th additions and contained more than half the land in what is now known as Manito Park. The 40-acre property eventually became the site of present-day Saint John's Episcopal Cathedral, as well as the home of the Episcopal Diocese on Thirteenth Avenue, purchased from Francis Cook in May 1907.

The life of the Cook family for the years following the sale of the *Spokan Times* is hard to document. These years were too early for the Spokane city directories, so there are no entries available to provide their residence at the time. There are, however, a few known facts:

1) Their first child, daughter Katharine, was born on November 11, 1881, in their home in the building that housed the newspaper at the corner of Riverside and Howard. She is the baby mentioned in the articles written about the Cook/Cannon affair.

2) The second child, daughter Laura May, was born on June 30, 1883. The newspaper had been sold a year before her birth.

3) The third child, son Silas Warren, was born on April 30, 1885. His obituary in the *Chronicle* of April 21, 1966, states: "He was born in 1876 in a two-story building on the southeast corner of Riverside and Howard where his father, Francis H. Cook, published Spokane's first newspaper." The obituary has a nine-year error in the birth date; it appeared to be incorrect about the birthplace as well. It was very doubtful the family was still residing in that building in 1885.

The forty-acre purchase listed above was recorded in May of 1884, another example of land being recorded at a date some time after the purchase. There is evidence that even while he was editing the *Times*, Francis was improving his property on the hill. He was also either building or remodeling a small house on the site where the family was going to live. They were living there at least by January 26, 1884, when the following article appeared in the *Spokane Falls Review*:

> Francis H. Cook is manufacturing ice on a large scale *at his place south of town* [emphasis added]. He is trying an experiment in the ice packing business that carries success on the face of it. He has a large number of five-gallon oil cans, which he fills with water and allows them to freeze. The cubes of ice are taken out when solidified and stacked together. Over this cold monument he will build a house [an icehouse] on the first indication of spring, and as he has any amount of materials the expense will be light. Mr. Cook will by this means be prepared to furnish the consumers with a pure article of ice next summer.

An article from the *Spokane Falls Review*, dated February 16, 1884, provides the following information (condensed):

SPOKANE HEIGHTS
The Future Building Spot for Wealthy Spokaneites

> To the south of Spokane Falls and hedging it in like a battlement, stretches a bluff that takes its source among the auriferous mountains of the Coeur d'Alene to the east of us and stretches with a grand sweep to the west until it terminates abruptly with the chasm that marks the course of the brawling Hangman's creek. It will in time to come be known as Spokane Heights and will be dotted and crowned with elegant suburban residences and villas. It is to-day valuable as building property, and will be much more so a few years hence.

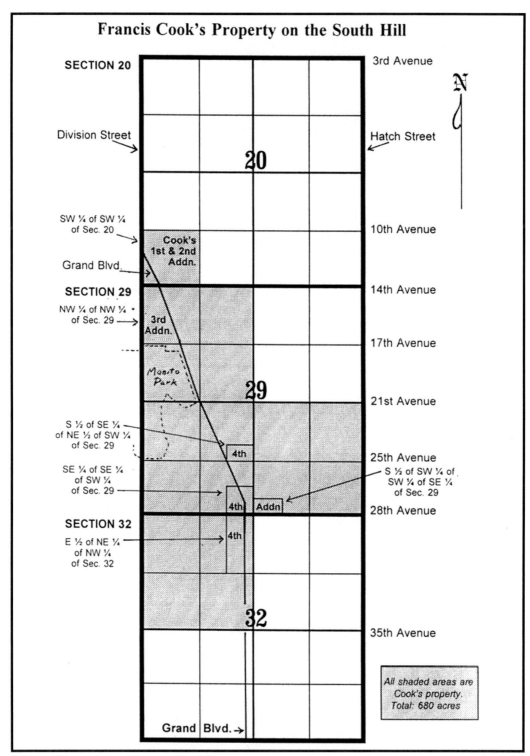

Francis Cook's Property on the South Hill

SECTION 20

Division Street →

3rd Avenue

Hatch Street ←

20

SW ¼ of SW ¼
of Sec. 20 →

10th Avenue

Cook's
1st & 2nd
Addn.

Grand Blvd. →

14th Avenue

SECTION 29

NW ¼ of NW ¼
of Sec. 29 →

3rd
Addn.

17th Avenue

Manito
Park

29

21st Avenue

S ½ of SE ¼
of NE ½ of SW ¼
of Sec. 29

4th

25th Avenue

S ½ of SW ¼ of
SW ¼ of SE ¼
of Sec. 29

SE ¼ of SE ¼
of SW ¼
of Sec. 29 →

4th Addn

28th Avenue

SECTION 32

E ½ of NE ¼
of NW ¼
of Sec. 32 →

4th

32

35th Avenue

All shaded areas are
Cook's property.
Total: 680 acres

Grand Blvd. →

Map of Francis and Laura Cook's properties on the South Hill. This area also included a portion of Manito Park where the first fair in the history of Spokane County was conducted. They owned a total of 680 acres on the South Hill, as designated in grey.

(This map was compiled and drawn by Doris Woodward.)

From almost the base, reaching to the summit and back over the higher ground for over a mile stretches the property of Francis H. Cook, Esq. Mr. Cook has resided in this place several years. He is a printer and editor by profession, and had the honor of running the first daily in this city. He made a success of this venture, but he cultivated a taste for farming and secured 40 acres on the bluff *in early days* [emphasis added]. To his original acres he added a section which brings his property up to 680 acres, every acre of which adjoins the city proper. [The last statement is misleading. He did purchase 640 acres from the Northern Pacific, which is the size of a section of land, but his purchases were actually portions of two sections.]

He has applied himself to the improvement and development of his property. He is an enthusiastic experimentist [*sic*], and has been fortunately successful in everything he has undertaken. He sent east for a saw mill outfit, put it up, and had it in working order before he called in a practical engineer to examine the work, who pronounced it perfect. Cook is running it now, getting out lumber for his own use, for his neighbors, and for the market.

He has sent east for all of the rarest and best-improved varieties of small fruits and vegetables, and in stock he has been just as particular, having imported the best breeds known to stock raisers at a large expense, but the wisdom of the investment is apparent in the magnificent growth of the animals. His water system is perfect, with springs of sufficient capacity to supply the entire city. One of the largest has been walled up and the water conducted in pipes to the residence, mill and all over the premises. He next will go into the ice business extensively next season. He floods the ice house to a depth of six inches, and when it is frozen, repeats the process until he has a solid monument of cold comfort.

Mr. Cook is always engaged upon some improvement scheme and is generally well rewarded in his undertakings. It is the intention of Mr. Cook *next year to put up an elegant and costly residence on the site of his present abode* [emphasis added].

There is a remarkable amount of information in the above article, which is much longer than what is printed here, solving some of the questions that have arisen about Francis Cook in the years following the sale of the *Times*. The date confirms the fact he was in possession of 680 acres and had been for some time, even though some of that land was not recorded until a later date. The newspaper article confirms this. It is probable Cook had an agreement with the Northern Pacific, giving him possession before the deeds were actually filed. It seems plausible the railroad would have been amenable to any reasonable agreement in order to sell its property.

The article also answers the previously controversial accounts of where the Cooks finally lived during the 1880s, some of which assumed they had moved directly from the building at Riverside and Howard into the "big house on the hill." It also gives credibility to an interview taken many years later by Louis Livingston, a Spokane history teacher and the director of the Cheney Cowles Museum (see Appendix II for more on Mr. Livingston), with the Cooks' fourth child, Clara, who was born January 12, 1887. When asked whether she was born in the big house, she answered:

No. I'm pretty sure I wasn't [born in that house]. I think I was born when they owned *the little house down the hill* [emphasis added]. I have no recollection of the first house I lived in, but I remember when they were building the new home – the noise of the carpenters and the Scotch-man that was always singing as he was pounding nails. That was my first recollection of the home.

What Clara meant by the "little house down the hill" isn't exactly known, but it was to this small house Francis moved his family, probably soon after he sold the paper or maybe even earlier. Clara also mentioned that her father had a sawmill during those years. She said, "It could have been down towards Browne's Addition," and added that she thought much of his money came from that source.

Solving the questions about Francis Cook's land purchases helps to determine the whereabouts of the Cook family after 1882 and provides an answer to questions about the birthplaces of some of the Cook children. Silas was certainly not born in the downtown building, and it is unlikely that the second child, Laura May, was born there either.

However, when the newspaper said the big house was to be built "on the site of the present abode," it cannot be taken literally, as the family was living in a "little house" while the big house was being built, undoubtedly nearby. Clara was probably correct in saying it was "down the hill." At any rate, it was close enough for her to hear the carpenters. This also gives a tentative date for the building of the big house. It is doubtful Clara remembered anything before she was three years old, indicating the big house was not built before 1890. No exact dates have been found for the actual building.

As indicated in the newspaper article, Francis was an ardent farmer. He approached this new occupation with his customary all-out effort. "His ice manufacturing business was very successful, as was the sawmill, and both contributed income that eventually enabled him to build the big house." But that was for a later time. Meanwhile—he was planning to hold a fair.

The First Agricultural Fair

Francis Cook, the eternal innovator, wasn't satisfied with being "just a farmer." He had the land, the imagination, and the determination to present to the people of Spokane their first agricultural fair. It was a huge undertaking and, in the annals of Spokane history, Cook's contribution in this area has often been overlooked.

A 1997 *Spokesman-Review* article covering Spokane's fairs printed the following: "An account of the first fair in Spokane, which began as an event of the Washington-Idaho Fair Association in 1886, was originally held at what we now know as

Corbin Park. One of its most prominent draws was horse racing." This is not correct. There may have been some horse racing at what became Corbin Park, but that would not have constituted a "fair." An actual racetrack was built at Corbin Park, but not until 1887, just in time for the second annual fair.

The follow image, scanned from the September 18, 1886, issue of the *Morning Review,* shows the headlines exactly as they appeared:

The 1887 *Spokane Falls Directory* includes the following listing (shown below): "Washington Fair Association (F. H. Cook, pres.) grounds one mile south of the city." Excitement about this affair was evident earlier in the summer of 1886. The *Morning Review* of August 6th was complimentary, emphasizing Cook "was working morning, noon and night for the success of the undertaking. The races will be among the best ever seen in this part of the country." It added Francis had gotten special rates from the railroad for the trips from Pasco, Yakima, Wallula and Heron.

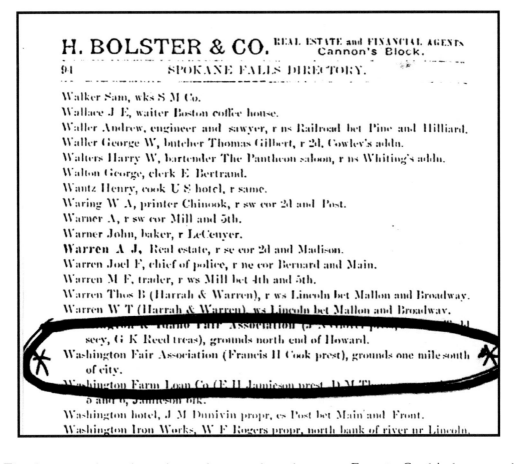

The fair must have been located somewhere between Francis Cook's home and what became Manito Park. The location had to be changed during the planning stage, but the newspaper was encouraging and applauded Cook for his efforts in undertaking such a difficult project. The paper mentioned an exhibition building and a racetrack, adding the weather was very dry, and the grounds were dusty, so racing was not as good as it might have been. On September 18th, the *Morning Review* closed their article with the following:

> We trust that our people will lend their presence to the fair every day and do all in their power to make it as much of a success as possible under existing circumstances.

The program for each day was ambitious and included the following events, among others: single driving horses, carriage teams, and saddle horses; shooting with shotguns and rifles; trotting and running; lady equestrians; and a parade of winning livestock before the grand stand. There was something for everyone. Entries for the events came from all over Eastern Washington—Colfax, Davenport, Farmington and Colville—as well as from North Idaho. On the second day of the fair, the *Morning Review* added some interesting information:

> The Management has spent $2,000 in laying pipes and excellent spring water is furnished to all parts of the grounds. A number of persons from distant parts of the country are attending with their families and are camped on the grounds. As the fair is now running, it promises to grow each day until the close.

Horse racing was the most popular, and with true Francis Cook humanitarianism, he outlawed the use of spurs and whips. However, racing also proved to be the most troublesome. The *Northwest Tribune* of Cheney reported on September 30, 1886:

> All things must have their commencement, and the East Washington Fair has made its little bow. Everybody can talk, but certainly it is a much better showing than Cheney made last year. The trouble in this matter has been the same trouble that enters every enterprise. Whiskey tried to run the fair, and because Mr. Cook is a temperance man and would not allow a saloon on the ground, a number of Spokane whiskey cranks sought to injure him by throwing discredit upon the fair.

Of particular interest in the above is the fact Francis Cook was a temperance man. It says much for the quality of this man, who would never sacrifice his beliefs for the sake of making money. The fair was not without faults, but it was an ambitious effort on the part of the indomitable Francis Cook.

Land Development and the Spokane and Montrose Railroad

With the close of the fair, Francis was able to turn his energies to working his farm, developing his property, and planning for the building of the new home. On January 12, 1887, just three and a half months after the close of the fair, Laura gave birth to their fourth child, Clara. She was busy indeed with her four children, the oldest being only five years old. One can imagine she was anticipating with pleasure moving into a larger home.

It was not long after this, in July 1887, that a newcomer arrived in town by the name of T. J. Dooley. He was an attorney who came from Minnesota, where he had been involved in real estate development. He was attracted to the young city of Spokane, especially to the property owned by Francis Cook. He quickly realized the advantages of developing property outside the city limits where city taxes would not be a deterrent.

On November 19th, Dooley and Cook formed a land-development partnership. In looking ahead to the importance of developing his property, Francis had recognized the need to have some method of transportation to get people from downtown Spokane to the South Hill. This was becoming important in other areas of the city as well. It was to be Dooley's responsibility to procure a franchise from the city for the construction of a motorized streetcar line and to arrange for funding. Cook's part in the plan was to build and maintain the streetcar operation. They also agreed Dooley would plat the land into residential lots, to be called the Montrose Addition, including streets, alleys, boulevards (Grand and Manito), and parks. Cook gave Dooley sole control over the sales, for which Dooley would receive twenty per cent for each lot sold. It was a three-year contract.

Cook, Dooley and two other men, Horatio Belt (future Spokane mayor) and E. A. Routhe, were granted a franchise on December 20, 1887, for constructing the motor line. Unfortunately, T. J. Dooley felt Cook was moving too slowly in beginning work on the streetcar line and initiated a lawsuit against him to get things moving. Horatio Belt had procured a $25,000 loan from the Provident Trust Company. The money was given to Cook, and Dooley was disturbed work hadn't yet begun. The two also had differences of opinion about the development of the land and the platting of lots. Evidently, Francis Cook wanted part of his land set aside for a park. Dooley may not have agreed with him, but that is mere speculation. Apparently the two men finally reached a mutual understanding, and construction of the motor trolley began in April 1888.

The Spokane & Montrose Motor Railroad Company was the first motor streetcar in Spokane. Another line had already been started between the city and Browne's Addition to transport residents and employees from downtown to the new mansions and houses being built west of town. These first streetcars were horse-drawn and the operation was successful except for the unpleasant problems involved in using horses.

Cook's first trolley was powered by a wood-burning steam engine and hauled two coaches for passengers. The engine and its coaches made the first trip on November 7, 1888. The railway had narrow-gauge tracks, and after the completion of the Washington Street viaduct under the railroad tracks, the route moved south on Washington from between Front Street (now Spokane Falls Boulevard) and Riverside. Halfway up the hill, it turned southeast, moving up to the present-day Rockwood Boulevard (now just south of Sacred Heart Hospital). Continuing east to a point where the Rockwood gateposts are now located, it switched to go west on Sumner (which was then called Prospect Avenue) to reach Grand Boulevard, still hardly more than a dirt road. From that point (the present location of St. John's Episcopal Cathedral), it continued south. The first line ended at about 19th Avenue, later extending to the car barns at 37th Avenue.

Spokane's first trolley line, founded in 1886 by H. C. Marshall and A. J. Ross, made its first trip in April of 1888. Its function was mainly to promote real estate development in Browne's Addition. Pictured above are driver Bill Shannon, conductor John Simonson and city council members taking their first ride. *(Photo from the Jerome Peltier Collection, courtesy Tony and Suzanne Bamonte)*

Cook's original Spokane and Montrose Motor Railroad, circa 1889, on Washington Street, just south of Spokane's first viaduct, which provided passage under the Northern Pacific Railroad tracks. When the line began operations, the viaduct was not yet completed. *(E. E. Bertrand photo, courtesy MAC L86-1040)*

This article appeared in the *Morning Review* of September 17, 1888:

THE MOTOR LINE
Public Gratification at its Early Completion
Comments on the Magnificent Suburban Property
The Trial Trip Yesterday—A Full Description of the Comfortable Jaunt—In Perspective

"All aboard!" shouted Conductor Peebles yesterday, and as the guests stepped on the car, the engine gave a tug and the long-delayed trip on the motor line was fairly under way.

HOPES REALIZED

For several weeks the streetcar line has been waiting for the Northern Pacific's permission to tunnel under the tracks at the Washington street crossing. At last, however, the owner of the city road, Mr. Cook, decided to operate his line at once as far as it is already completed. He issued a number of invitations for the trip and among those who accepted them were: Mayor Hoover and wife; Councilmen Water, Johnson and Fotheringham; J. J. White, city clerk; Chief Warren; City Attorney Houghton; and the representatives of the press.

THE ROUTE

The heavy haul of so many passengers up the steep grade along the four blocks on Washington street severely tested the power of the motor; but after a sharp struggle she mounted the hill and turned her face to the East. The engine that drew the first car over the line is a very powerful one of forty-horse power with six drive wheels, which are good at holding or propelling. The line runs from there to Stevens street, and after winding in and out for some distance, enters a deep rock cut about 200 feet long. Emerging from this cut the road traverses the side of a high bluff, from which a grand view of the city is obtainable.

PICTURESQUE SCENERY

Ascending another grade we reached the switchback and mounted to the summit of the hill [the site of the present Cathedral of St. John]. From there the road continues on for one mile through Montrose Park and other additions to our city. The land there is level prairie with the best of soil instead of the gravel upon which the city proper is built, and the residences [residential] property in that neighborhood will now become quite as attractive as that in any other part of town.

When the end of the line was reached the guests stepped out of the car and were engaged for some time looking at the scenery; and they would have probably kept on gazing until nightfall if the whistle had not warned them to get aboard for the return trip, which was made in very quick time.

As they stepped off the car at Second street the passengers with one accord thanked Mr. Cook for his courtesy and the ride, and sauntered to their respective homes.

The crew of the train were: Conductor, Cad Peebles; engineer, Frank Goodrich; fireman, John Krick. The regular schedule will be in operation tomorrow. The line will be run with a transfer at the Washington street crossing to one of the company's cars which will be pulled by horses to the Front street end of the road [the Washington Street viaduct was not completed when the streetcar began operating].

Downtown Spokane in 1888 before the streetcars. *(Photo from* Spokane and the Inland Empire *by N. W. Durham, 1912)*

The entire operation was a huge one for Francis Cook to undertake. The line was popular and succeeded in bringing people into the Montrose Park subdivision, but there was little profit for Cook. The first steam engine proved troublesome, so Francis electrified the line in 1892, buying the electricity from the Washington Water Power Company. This was one of the first electrified streetcars in Spokane. According to Francis's wife Laura, the cost of adapting the system to electricity was $30,000.

During this time, he continued to work his farm and made plans for building the new house. This is what Laura and the children had been waiting for. Francis and Laura also had the pleasure of welcoming his twin brother, Frank, to Spokane.

Franklin Pierce Cook

Frank Cook arrived with his family sometime in the late 1880s. According to Frank's obituary in the *Spokesman-Review* on February 16, 1933, his brother persuaded him to come to Spokane from Tacoma by offering him "three tracts of land, which now constitute a large part of what is the Rockwood addition." It was a wonderful opportunity for Frank, who moved with his wife, Emma, and their two children, Mary and Norman. It had been several years since the twin brothers had seen each other.

Frank Cook became the first superintendent of his brother's street railway and by 1890 was the conductor of one of the two steam cars. The conductor of the other car was Peter Mertz, who became his good friend. Frank is first found in the 1889 *Spokane City Directory* as being in real estate. In 1891, in the first election after the new city charter was in force, Frank P. Cook was elected the councilman from the 1st Ward at the time David Fotheringham was mayor. His friend, Peter Mertz, was

The Trail of Francis Cook's Montrose Line

This remarkable drawing of Spokane Falls and Cook's motor line as seen from Spokane Heights was published in *The Northwest Magazine* in April 1890. The artist's name as signed in the lower left was C. Winsor, '90

It illustrates the journey of Cook's trolley from downtown to a height 350 feet above. It shows the Washington Street railroad viaduct, under which the trolley went south to about Sixth Avenue, where it wound its way through the lower South Hill, turning east, then south, then east again, where it joined a street that led south to Rockwood Boulevard.

In those years, the portion that angled southeast on Rockwood Boulevard was called Hill Street, and it went to a point where it joined Tenth Avenue. At that spot, the trolley was turned around to go up Prospect Avenue, traveling steeply upward to reach what is now Grand Boulevard.

Prospect Avenue is now called Sumner Avenue, and the route can still be taken by automobile for anyone who is interested.

In the picture one can see the houses that Frank Cook built, one of which he lived in, and the house in the center at the bottom is Francis and Laura Cook's. That property is now the site of St. John's Cathedral. The present Jewett House stands where the Cook home was located. The two-car trolley can be seen as it was turning onto Grand.

Spokane Falls – View of Cook's motor line from Spokane Heights, elevation 350 feet.

The trail of Francis Cook's Montrose line.

Cook's first wood-fired steam engine shown in a rock cut on its first trip in 1888. From left: Ed Nelson, fireman; Frank LeDuc, engineer; Peter Mertz, conductor, also later became Spokane's sixth police chief, 1891-1895; and two unidentified boys. *(Photo courtesy MAC, L86-1049)*

by that time the chief of police. By 1892, the Frank Cook family was living at 102 East Hill Avenue. This was a short street bordering Rockwood Boulevard and down the hill from Sumner Avenue. It was in the same area where Francis was building his big house, so they were close neighbors.

There is some interesting information about the Frank Cook family in the 1900 Spokane census. Frank Cook's children, who were both in their twenties, are also listed as living at 102 East Hill Avenue, although they are not on the same page with their parents. Also, at what appears to be the same address, there were four Chinese residents: a gardener, a truck gardener, and two garden laborers. Since Frank didn't own a farm, these Chinese may have been working for Francis Cook on his farm.

Frank and Emma's children went to work not long after their arrival in Spokane. Norman graduated from South Central High School (later became Lewis & Clark)

Franklin Pierce Cook and his wife, Emma Berkey Cook. *(Photo courtesy Cook family)*

and became an abstractor for a title company for several years. Mary was a stenographer. Both of them usually lived with their parents, although Norman also had a place of his own for a while.

Frank and Emma moved from their home on Hill Avenue to 2015 South Grand Avenue, across from Manito Park. By 1909, they had moved to the Kempis Apart-

Kempis Apartments at Sixth and Washington. *(Photo by Doris Woodward)*

ments at Sixth Avenue and Washington. That building is still there. Frank was also involved in other businesses during his stay in Spokane and is found in various city directories. In 1893, he was a collector for the internal revenue. In 1903 and 1904, he worked in brick manufacturing, and from 1908 through 1912, he was a deputy county assessor. He appears to have been a man of many talents, not unlike his twin brother.

Frank's wife Emma died on December 21, 1916. She is buried at Riverside Memorial Park, in a grave not too far distant from Francis and Laura Cook. By 1918, Frank and his children were no longer in Spokane. They moved to Juneau, Alaska, where Frank was involved in prospecting. In the 1930 Juneau census, he is living alone, age 78, and is called a "placer miner." Frank died in Juneau on February 14, 1933, at age 82. In his obituary, printed in the *Spokesman-Review* on February

16th, Peter Mertz said about his friend: "Frank built three houses south of the big reservoir on Rockwood Boulevard. Two of them are still standing." Both of Frank's children, Norman and Mary Cook, married in Alaska and died there.

One of the more delightful details of Franklin Pierce Cook's life came from a granddaughter, who described him as being very proper and always wore a black bow tie, very similar to descriptions of his twin brother, Francis.

The House on the Hill

No evidence has been found to determine just when Francis and Laura's house was started, how much it cost, or who designed it. There were architects in Spokane at that time who were doing good work for the *nouveau riche* in town. It is not unreasonable, however, to suppose Francis Cook acted as his own architect. As he is known to have been very competent in so many different endeavors, it wouldn't be surprising to find he had done the job himself.

It is not known when the building of the house began, but because of the *Northwest Magazine* article, we know the house was finished by April 1890. By 1891, Laura had given birth to two more children, both boys. Frank Arthur Cook was born on September 2, 1888, and Chester Robert Cook arrived on July 12, 1890, so the Cook family was indeed ready for a new home. The one Francis created for them was beautiful.

In Louis Livingston's interview with Clara, we are fortunate to have a wonderful description of this grand home. In her words:

> It was a huge home. We had four lovely, great, big parlors on the first floor and then there was a large conservatory and a large dining room with a dumb waiter that came up from the kitchen. I had many a ride in that dumb waiter. Then we went on up to the second floor, and I don't remember how many great big bedrooms. I do remember in the front part of the house with windows all around, there was a beautiful maple dinner table, and the neighbors used to come up the hill to play so often.
>
> And then we had another floor too I guess you'd call it a steeple or a tower. We would run about that. We kids thought that was a lot of fun because we could make all the noise we wanted, and it had a railing all around it ... and you could see all over town. ... This home also had that porch that went all the way around it with a railing. We had a little yellow dog and we used to run around that, I remember, and it was a lot of fun.
>
> We always had at least two people to help. I remember Mother always liked these Swedish maids, and I didn't because I had curly hair and they were always pulling my curls. She [mother] always had to have help because we had quite a family by this time.

Livingston asked Clara, "You said something about there being a reservoir in front of the house?" She responded:

A view of the houses on Hill Avenue below Francis Cook's new home. Frank Cook built the three identical houses below his brother's home. Frank and his family lived in the one on the right. The tracks for the trolley line, which ran between the poles, are barely visible. *(Photo courtesy Cook family)*

Well, father also owned this spring that was way back in the same territory with Manito Park and he piped that to Cook's Addition to all of the people and we collected rent off of them too. ...This reservoir was for storage of water that was piped from way out at Manito so that there would be enough pressure for the irrigation and so on and so forth. It was underground mostly. That is, it was built on the side hill and I remember the fear of being near it and warned by my parents never to go near that and don't open the door. I could hear the water splash. ... It was down in the yard; yes, down the hill. I don't know how they did that.

[We lived there] a good many years. I have a picture of it [the house] when I was about, I guess, five or six years old. I was on the porch; and then I remember a younger sister that was ten years younger than me or maybe fourteen years – no, she was about ten or twelve years younger than I am. I remember she was born on Thanksgiving Day, and I was a pretty good-sized girl going to school.

In an old paper found in Clara's Bible, she added the following additional details about the house:

The entrance to the house was very impressive, with its large entrance halls and beautiful stairway ... four large rooms, with two parlors and a library. In this library was a metal stand that supported a large leather Bible. Father was an impressive reader and, though I was very young, I loved to hear him read from the "big book" and pray to the Heavenly Father. The second floor had six bedrooms that I remember. Part of the house was only for company. The billiard room on the second floor was of great interest when friends came up the hill to play pool.

The Final Years on the South Hill

The days in the house on the hill were numbered, but the Cook family enjoyed it while they were there. Three more children were born during those years—all daughters: Edith Lee on February 2, 1892; Lolita Evelyn on November 13, 1893; and Florence Helene on November 26, 1896. Florence was the "Thanksgiving Day baby" referred to in Clara's interview and was the last child to be born in the house on the South Hill. The children now numbered nine.

Francis Cook's plans for the Montrose development were ambitious and involved more expense than he had foreseen, as did the streetcar project. In addition, furnishing the house must also have been an enormous expense. Entirely out of Cook's hands was the Panic of 1893, followed by a serious nationwide depression, which lasted for several years.

There were many causes for the Panic of 1893. The United States had enjoyed remarkable economic expansion in the 1880s, but much of it was driven by speculation. Railroads were vastly over-built; droughts in the Midwest resulted in the failure of crops and farms; and the drop in the price of silver affected all the country, particularly the Inland Northwest. There was an immediate run on banks—many throughout the country and in Spokane failed. Some of Spokane's most affluent businessmen lost everything. So did Francis Cook. Many of them filed for bankruptcy, but Francis didn't believe in it. He sold everything to satisfy his creditors.

The Cook mansion at 1227 South Grand. *(Photo courtesy Cook family)*

Francis and Laura Cook with six of their eleven children in 1890. Left to right: Clara, Francis, Frank, Katie, Laura holding baby Chester, Silas and Laura May. *(Photo courtesy Cook family)*

In her article of August 3, 1933, Laura Cook wrote an account about the critical events of 1893. Laura has been found to be honest and forthright in her reporting of their earlier life and times and appears to be correct in her evaluation of what happened following the 1893 panic:

> When the depression came in 1894, Mr. Cook turned over his home, streetcar line and property in which now is called Manito to satisfy mortgage companies. Some persons failed to meet their obligations to him and money could not be obtained to carry on. He was advised to put our home in my name, but that was contrary to his sense of justice.

> He preferred rather to lose his property than his good name. It was reported he had been offered $1,000,000 for his holdings. If business had not been ruined temporarily, he would no doubt have realized his expectations. It now is one of the finest residential districts in Spokane. Mr. Cook was far-sighted. It was not through poor judgment that he had lost. Conditions were beyond his control.

> Mr. Cook had faith in Spokane and he labored incessantly for the well being of the town, which later fulfilled his fondest dreams. He gave liberally of his means during the early days to encourage the building of schools, churches and railroads or any enterprise for the general good of the city.

Daughter Clara, remembering those times in the interview with Livingston, had this to say about her father and the Panic of '93:

> Father got quite involved with giving away everything to everybody that had bought land of him ... they used his lumber, his sawmill, and they all owed him so much, and so he wrote on their mortgages "Paid In Full." ... He was broken-hearted over everything, went into debt himself. At the time before he passed away, the man that foreclosed on him came to see him, and I remember seeing this man crying and telling father how sorry he was that he had brought this on him when he had done so much for everybody else. Father said, "Well, that's what makes it easy for me to come in the presence of my Maker right now. I have no regrets." [Francis's wife later recalled that the man's name was Reider.]

From *Manito Park: A Reflection of Spokane's Past* by Tony and Suzanne Bamonte, we find the following description of Cook's difficulties:

> Cook suffered the loss of his Spokane & Montrose streetcar company. He also lost the land offered as collateral on the $40,000 note in a sheriff's sale in 1895 (Superior Court case #8425). Most of Cook's dreams for the future of the development of the Montrose/Manito neighborhood and park were swallowed up with the loss of the land. However, records indicate Cook made every effort to retain possession of their elegant home by selling much of their property adjacent to their home. Sadly, their efforts were futile. In July of 1897, the house was lost to the Provident Trust company in another sheriff's sale. Soon after, it became a sanitarium for the Seventh-day Adventists.

Planning for a park on his property was now out of his hands. It was left for others to actually accomplish this, but it began with Francis's dream. It would be another decade before it would come to fruition, with the eventual creation of Spokane's most famous landmark, Manito Park, a large portion of which lies on Cook's former property between 17th and 25th avenues.

The question arises as to what happened to T. J. Dooley during this period. The only records available are the city directories, and Mr. Dooley is found only in the 1888 directory, as a lawyer. It appears he did what he wanted with Francis Cook's property and then left town. There may have been extenuating circumstances for his exodus, but to date no records have surfaced to explain it.

Major changes lay ahead for the Cook family, but there is no evidence any of the children or their parents resented this upheaval in their lives. As Clara said later about her parents: "They were wonderful people and they lived their religion. There was no smoking, drinking, carousing, or anything ... It was a lovely memory of mother and father, never a cross word ever." They were a strong family, and they were together. That was the important thing.

With his usual fortitude, Francis Cook moved on with his life and took care of his wife and children. His business dealings with the City of Spokane were, for the most part, at an end.

The present Manito duck pond, formerly called Mirror Lake, circa 1925. *(Photo courtesy Spokane Parks and Recreation Department)*

THE CREATION OF MANITO PARK

When Francis Cook chose to surrender his South Hill property to his creditors rather than face bankruptcy, his hopes for the creation of a park were gone. Fortunately for Spokane, however, the idea was not lost, and even though Cook's personal dream was not fulfilled, a park did emerge that is a showcase for Spokane.

A brief history of the period finds the following: The Northwestern & Pacific Hypotheekbank foreclosed on the $40,000 promissory note, which the Cooks had executed on July 19, 1892, putting up about 460 acres in the Montrose Park area as collateral. This property included all of the acreage that Cook hoped to turn into a park. Jay P. Graves, with a newly acquired mining fortune, purchased Cook's Spokane & Montrose Railroad Company, which became the nucleus of the Spokane Traction Company. It provided Graves with his initial foothold in the Montrose Park area. The Provident Trust Company and Washington Water Power were other creditors who benefited from Francis Cook's misfortune.

Graves's newly created Spokane-Washington Improvement Company was organized for land development in the area. He and his brother Will had the foresight to develop and promote what was at that time still referred to as "Montrose Park," and they soon began the promotion of what was now called the "Manito Addition." The boundaries were the same as Francis Cook's—north to south from 14th Avenue to 33rd, and east to west from Hatch Street to Division. Graves also improved his Spokane & Montrose railway line in 1902 by providing better cars and standard gauge tracks.

There was abundant evidence that land development was improved tremendously by having a nearby park, and they quickly took advantage of Francis Cook's initial plan. Graves's next step was to organize the adjacent property owners to donate 95 acres to the city to be used as a park. The city in turn agreed to build a road system through the new park and a main waterline. In 1903, the name became officially "Manito Park."

Graves's plans were momentous for the city and financially profitable for him. They provided a new boom in real estate for the area. His plans were also a validation of Francis Cook's foresight many years before. It is important to remember that Cook was the first owner of South Hill property on the Manito plateau, which had the potential of being very valuable. He could easily have subdivided all of his property with the promise of an excellent return on his initial investment. Instead, he withheld a large portion of it, about 45-50 acres, from subdivision for the use of a future park. It is Spokane's good fortune that he chose to do this. Had he not, Manito Park would probably not exist today. It is also fortunate that Jay P. Graves and the other creditors concurred with Francis Cook's original plan and fulfilled his dream as he might never have been able to do. Many people have contributed over the years to the development of this unique place and have left Spokane with a one-of-a-kind city park, renowned throughout the country—thanks initially to Francis H. Cook.

The bandstand, built in 1908, was at the peak of the hill northeast of the present Park Bench Cafe. *(Libby Studio photo, courtesy MAC 2309)*

Mirror Lake

What is now called the Manito duck pond was originally a much larger lake in that portion of Francis Cook's property that he proposed to set aside for a park. It was in a relatively wild and rocky area that abounded in roses and other wild flowers. Cook envisioned this area, which he called Montrose Park ("mountain of roses"), as a place where everyone in the community could spend their leisure time with picnics, games and hikes.

E. Charles Balzer was hired as the first superintendent of the park and served in that position until his resignation in 1909. He was a florist by profession and was instrumental in developing the plantings at the park. The lake was a troublesome factor during much of that time. A narrow portion of the lake extended as far east as Grand Boulevard, and during the summer months portions of it dried up, becoming stagnant and mosquito-infested. Manito Park had several springs, which were used advantageously. There exist a few letters that Balzer wrote to the Board of Park Commissioners in 1908, which give some insight into the work done previously by Francis Cook. A portion of Balzer's letter of July 12, 1908, gives the following information:

Regarding the water going down Grand, [I] will say that 4 years ago when we first started [working on] the lake, we looked up all the spring water we could find; we found a spring in the Manito Blvd. This spring went to the old Cook's Hospital piped in a 3-inch iron pipe. We cut this pipe where our present spring is and led the water through the fountain, then we found that Cook had put in 8-inch sewer tiles to drain the bottom where our present improvements are.

Mirror Lake, now known as the duck pond. *(Photo courtesy Bill Stewart)*

The heart of the Manito Park zoo established by park superintendent E. Charles Balzer in 1905. *(Libby Studio photo, courtesy MAC L87-1.771.04)*

The foregoing furnishes some answers as to how and where Francis Cook procured the water to fill his reservoir and irrigate his land. Clara Cook, in her interview with Louis Livingston, mentioned that water was furnished to the newly built homes in that area as well.

Other Developments

Balzer also had ambitious plans for the park. He wanted to enlarge the lake, making it of more use for ice skating in the winter and boating and swimming in the summer. He anticipated that the tons of black soil retrieved from enlarging the lake would be put on the rocky hills. One of his more delightful ideas was to erect a lookout house on the top of the "big hill," two stories high and with a large flag pole. According to Balzer: "A person can see Post Falls from this hill on a clear day and will overlook the whole city." This big hill was undoubtedly the great rocky knoll that stands between 17th and 18th avenues near the park entrance, which at that time was called Flag Hill.

Charles Balzer's career as superintendent came to a close when a nonpartisan park board commission was formed in 1907, largely due to the influence of Aubrey L. White, taking the control of the parks out of the hands of the city. White wanted as park superintendent a man more experienced in planning and laying out the new developments. Balzer had done a good job, often under very difficult conditions, and the popularity of Manito Park had flourished during that time. He had accomplished many things, sometimes at his own cost, and deserves to be remembered for those beginning efforts.

The next superintendent was John W. Duncan, an exceptional man who served at Manito Park for 32 years and was instrumental in developing the park to its present glory. Noted features of the park today include the Duncan Gardens, Rose Hill, and the Lilac Garden, areas dedicated to some of the people who were important in the growth of Manito Park—John W. Duncan, Dr. David Gaiser and Joel E. Ferris, among others. A major impact on the development of the park came in 1990, with the founding of the Friends of Manito. The activities of this voluntary, non-profit group have been instrumental in maintaining, developing and preserving the quality of Manito Park.

Two little girls walking in the Duncan Garden at Manito Park. *(Photo courtesy Tony and Suzanne Bamonte)*

The last area to be developed to date was the Japanese Garden on the west side of Manito Park. Dedicated on May 17, 1974, it was named the Nishinomiya Japanese Garden to commemorate Spokane's sister city in Japan. In 2007, the name was changed to the Nishinomiya-Tsutakawa Japanese Garden to honor Spokane artist and businessman Ed Tsutakawa, who first suggested the idea of having a sister city. Tsutakawa, along with former Mayor Neal Fosseen and his wife, Helen, were instrumental in establishing the sister city relationship between Spokane and Nishinomiya, thereby leaving a great legacy for future generations.

In addition to these renowned areas, one must not forget that there still are remote parts of the park, which are little known but still enjoyed by the dedicated hikers and dog walkers. It is not hard to find yourself in a completely isolated area, where you have the feeling that perhaps no one has ever been there before. It is a rare feature for a city park, where usually every square foot is easily seen and visited at all times. Not so with Manito Park—and it makes this a place of unique pleasure and enjoyment.

This is perhaps what enchanted Francis Cook the most when he first found himself the owner of this wonderful tract of land. With his customary foresight, he saw what it could become.

Section III
The Move North

The Little Spokane

Francis Cook may have been down, but he was not out. On December 8, 1887, he had the wisdom to purchase a section of land north of Spokane from the Northern Pacific Railroad, with a five-year contract of sale. Terms for the sale required him to make annual payments, beginning on December 8, 1888. Including interest, they equaled $2,619.14; the last payment was made on December 8, 1892. The Cooks were fortunate indeed that the last payment was made before the financial world collapsed.

Francis H. Cook
(Photo from a Spokane First National Bank advertisement)

The property he purchased was Section 5 of Township 26, and it lay 2¾ miles due north of the forty acres in his portion of Section 20. It was an excellent purchase and one that eventually became an important asset to the Spokane scene—embracing the future Wandermere Golf Course and the residential area around the Little Spokane River. Of more importance, it provided a place for the Cook family to move when they had to vacate their beautiful "house on the hill." The exact date of the move is not known, but it was sometime during 1897 or 1898.

The house they moved to was old and small and must have been a crowded home for the eleven Cook residents. The Little Spokane River was behind it, and near it was a small lake. Francis had big plans for the lake and its proximity to the Little Spokane River. Meanwhile, on November 22, 1898, Laura gave birth to their tenth child, daughter Winifred Josephine. This time there was no domestic help for her, but the older daughters were there to give her assistance. That was to be their responsibility in the coming years. Oldest son Silas found work in the area, hoping to help with the family finances.

Francis made the move with pleasure. He was grateful to be living a life outdoors. Daughter Clara especially made note of this fact and mentioned it several times in her interview with Louis Livingston.

> He had such a busy life from the time he was sixteen years old when he started to make his own way, and he loved it out in the open … he used to get us up real early [in the] morning. He used to say, "Get up and hear the birds sing." He just loved the open spaces. He loved anything out in the open.

Laura provides the best account of their early life on the Little Spokane. She said that Francis enlarged the lake to about seven acres and stocked it with trout, both eastern brooks and rainbows, the beginning of an important fish hatchery. One of his first projects was inventing a rock crusher. He set this up next to one owned by the city. It proved to be capable of crushing more rock with less power. This crushed rock was used for Spokane roads. He also invented "rolls" (rollers?) to work under smaller rock crushers, many of which were sold for assaying purposes.

It was apparent that even with all the reverses and hard luck of the recent years, Francis and Laura both had the same determination to make their life and that of their children as pleasant and worthwhile as possible. They were indomitable!

There was no school in the immediate area. According to daughter Florence, Francis donated the land to the township to build a one-room schoolhouse. There were families in this northern area who must have been pleased to be able to send their children to a school closer to home, rather than having to transport them to the city. Cook's land adjoined that of W. H. Dart, who had homesteaded a portion of Section 6 in Township 26. Dart had a store not far from Cook's property where they were able to do necessary shopping.

Francis also became involved as a lawyer for a while, something brand new for him. Their closest neighbor was a Mr. Cushing. According to daughter Clara's account, Mr. Cushing got into an altercation with a disgruntled employee, who attacked Cushing with an iron rod. Cushing wrenched the rod away from the man, striking and killing him. Mr. Cushing was tried for murder, and his good friend and neighbor, Francis Cook, defended him in court. Up to this time, Francis Cook was never known to have any legal experience at all, but he did his best for his friend and was able to get the sentence reduced from the death penalty to life in prison.

This information is provided in daughter Clara's interview and, once again, it is a wonderful account of the Cooks' early years at the Little Spokane. She well remembered that their first home there was very small and not large enough for their family. "Father never really built a home the size that we needed," she said. Apparently they rented the Cushing place next door after Mr. Cushing went to prison. "It was a very nice house." In talking about those times, she added, "I remember going to the Court House in Spokane ... and hearing my father so eloquently defending this man [Cushing]. My father had a wonderful vocabulary and a wonderful ability to talk."

By early 1900, Francis was back to his usual optimistic self and was making plans for the lake he had started on his property. On May 1st, the *Chronicle* published the following (partially condensed):

Plans are being made for the construction of an artificial lake on the Little Spokane river, which will be three-quarters of a mile long, and one-quarter of a mile wide. On the banks of this will be a boat house and bathing houses, while in the lake itself will be hundreds of trout of all sizes.

F. H. Cook, who owns 600 acres of land on the Little Spokane river, a short distance above Dart's mill, is the person who is laying these plans. ... At present Mr. Cook owns one of the finest trout hatcheries in the state of Washington and his seven-acre lake swarms with from 30,000 to 50,000 fish, ranging in length from four to fourteen inches. Mr. Cook at present allows no fishing in his lake, but next year intends to throw it open to the public at a certain rate per pound.

The article continues by quoting exactly what Francis told the reporter:

TELLS OF HIS PLANS

I will not allow any fishing on my premises this summer. I have about 50,000 fish now in my lake, but I do not think it best to allow fishing this summer. Next summer I expect to be able to allow people to fish there at a certain rate per pound. I have not put any in my lake this spring, but am leaving the fish I have to themselves to increase.

There have been thousands of eastern brook trout hatched out this spring, but the native trout have only laid their eggs and will not hatch for about forty days. The chief work which I am doing this summer is the building of canals. I do this instead of throwing food to the fish. I do not believe in feeding them, as they should be kept as nearly as possible in their natural state. By building more canals there is more shore line and the small insects which lay eggs in water can be caught better by the fish. The lake is supplied with 1,000,000 gallons of fresh spring water a day. This is a large supply and far more than the fish need.

THE LAKE

I am going to make a lake on my property three-quarters of a mile wide. The way I intend doing this is to put a large high dam across the river. This will make one of the finest outing places near Spokane. I know Mr. Dart will make a fuss when I start building the dam, but it will be on my own private grounds and he can not possibly stop me. No, I do not expect to have a lawsuit with him in the proposition, but I will build my dam. I will try to commence work this fall, but may not be able to start until spring. [Francis had initiated a lawsuit against Mr. Dart on November 5, 1898, for building a similar dam, flooding part of the Cook property as a result. Francis lost that suit and evidently felt he was entitled to do the same thing farther up the river.]

After the lake is finished, I will build a fine beach for bathing and a good supply of row boats. I do not know yet whether I will have a steam launch or not, but probably will. There will also be other improvements put up which I have not yet decided upon. The land will then be rented to campers for the season. In my small lake I am sure I will have far more fish than I can take care of and will put a great many in the river. I want to help the public out all I can and keep good fishing in the stream. There will be no nets in the river and the fish once placed in it can roam where they will. I will not charge extra for fishing in the river, but a person renting a boat or having a camp will have the privilege of fishing free. If they want better fishing they can fish at the terms I mentioned in my upper lake. I think that I will purchase more land and enlarge the lake.

The mill I am building is nearly completed. I expect the machinery to arrive in the city this week and I will then put it in place and start the mill. It will cost all told about $2500. Not a large mill, but for what I want it is large enough. I want it to supply my own needs in building up my place. I built a large ice house with a capacity of 4000 tons on my place, but on account of the poor winter did not succeed in laying up any ice.

I feel no hesitancy in saying that in a comparatively short time we will have an electric line to the river. We have plenty of water power there to run an electric line that distance and I will make a strong effort to have a line built.

His ideas were ambitious and had tremendous possibilities. As was true with everything he did, his plans were well thought out and had the potential for success.

In the 1900 U.S. Census the Cook family is found in the Mayer Precinct, Spokane County. Francis is called a farmer; Laura and the ten children are all there. However, there are a couple of errors (not unusual in census returns). The baby is called "Dorothy," and Francis's father's birthplace is listed as Pennsylvania. It is not known who gave the erroneous information to the census taker, or perhaps he couldn't read his own handwriting!

The census was taken on the 8th and 9th of June. Four months later, the family gained another member. On October 9, 1900, the Cooks' eleventh and last child was born: Ralph Wheeler Cook. There were now four boys and seven girls. It appeared the Cook family was well on its way to a successful life on this 640-acre Little Spokane property.

The children were kept busy during those years. There were never-ending chores, of course, but also good times. The lake froze in the winter, perfect for ice-skating, and in the summer fishing provided the family with many good meals. The older boys helped with the ice business, hauling it to town from the big icehouse in an ice wagon with the sign "Cook's Spring Water Ice" blazoned on the side. The three oldest girls, Katharine, Laura and Clara, went to high school in Spokane; the younger children attended the local school.

Florence Cook, the ninth child, had early memories of those days, which she shared in an interview many years later. She remarked she had started first grade in the one-room schoolhouse, where her sister Kate (Katharine) was teaching, probably about 1902. The school was located on the Cooks' property "over the hill toward Dartford." According to Florence, she was a tease, often getting into mischief, and Kate told their mother, "Florence is spoiling my whole class." Consequently, she was taken out of school until the next year with a new teacher. The teachers usually boarded with the Cooks. Florence also recalled the family rarely went to church, because the trip into Spokane took so long. However, her mother for many years taught Sunday school in the schoolhouse, and the children from all around would come.

Florence's happiest recollections were of her parents:

> My mother was a wonderful woman. She and my father never quarreled. My father would get mad at my mother and he'd say, "Now don't get your Irish up." That would make her furious but she would never say a word. She'd go off in her bedroom. ... They were very religious people and my mother was very pious. We couldn't even say, "Darn it." We couldn't have cards in the house or anything, so my brothers always took the cards and played down by the barn. I never heard my father swear ever. The worst thing he ever said was "Great Scot!" ... That's the only swear word I ever heard him use. He never smoked. He never drank. He never cussed but he did say "Great Scot!" That was his swear word.

In 1902, Laura May married Austin Gubser at the First Presbyterian Church in Spokane. Three years later, Katharine Ruth married William Alvis at the family home, according to an article in the *Spokane Valley Herald* about 1950. First son, Silas, began working at sawmill logging. Clara, the historian of the family, had to leave high school when baby Ralph was born. She assisted her mother with the other children and helped do the cooking. Clara was able to start high school the following year, however, and she is found in the 1903 *Spokane City Directory*, a student, boarding at 1204 Sharp, the home of Judge and Mrs. Horatio Belt. She didn't finish her last year of high school. At age 19, she married Hugh Fuson. (For more detailed information concerning the Cook children, refer to Appendix II.)

Life was changing for the Cook family, and Francis never achieved his goal of establishing a summer resort in the area.

Mount Spokane
(Photo courtesy R. Morrison Photography)

It undoubtedly would have been a successful venture, but once more, his thoughts were moving elsewhere. He had become enchanted with a mountain––Mount Carlton, more commonly known as "Old Baldy," which he viewed every day from his farm and dreamed of what might be accomplished there. Soon, all his energy and thoughts were devoted to constructing a road to the top of this magnificent peak.

Cook's Mountain

Francis and son Silas took a trip to the top of the mountain not long after they moved to the Little Spokane and found the view to be magnificent. According to his wife, Laura, Francis was "a lover of nature and the great outdoors; it fascinated him." He had long felt there should be a road to the top of the mountain under municipal ownership but was unable to convince anyone else. According to Clyde Stricker in *Purchasing A Mountain*, as early as 1905 "Cook had organized a company to build a scenic, Swiss-type railroad up the west side of the mountain." It was a great idea, but as so often happened with Francis Cook, his ideas were ahead of the times and he was unable to generate support for his plan.

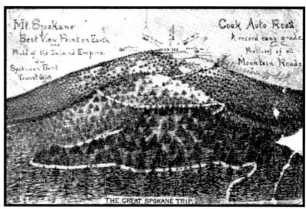

The writing on this card: Mount Spokane – Best Viewpoint on Earth, Pride of the Inland Empire. Also Spokane's Best Tourist Offer. Cook Auto Road. Prettiest of All Mountain Roads. *(Courtesy Cook family)*

In order to build a road, Francis realized that it would be necessary to purchase the top of the mountain. According to Silas in the *Spokane Daily Chronicle*, June 14, 1934:

> It was rumored the top of the mountain was to be purchased privately and a burro trail built up the Spirit Lake side. Father was much grieved, as the burro trail idea did not conform to his plans. He suggested to me that we go up and locate the corners of the school section, which took in the top of the mountain. Before we could go, winter snows set in. We drove as far as we could, left our horses and followed the old trail. After locating the corners, and with Spokane's welfare still in his heart, the land was advertised and purchased by my father in the winter of 1908.

> The next summer we spent looking for possible routes for a road. ... We decided on a route around the south slopes of Mount Spokane, made our location, purchased land from several homesteaders and from the Northern Pacific railway and cut out timber for a right of way for a couple of miles.

According to Silas, one of the homesteaders who had sold some land to Cook had a change of mind and later vehemently objected, gun in hand, causing the Cooks to change the route rather than lose their lives.

Laura recalled the many hardships faced and obstacles that had to be overcome: securing the rights-of-way, surveys and resurveys, and the short work season because

"There's Spokane!" Francis pointing to Spokane from the top of the mountain. The young girl is Florence, with brother Silas behind her. The other two younger women may be daughters but are not identified. The woman on the right could be Francis's wife. *(Photo courtesy Cook family)*

of early snow in fall and late snow in spring. The extensive rock formations made construction very difficult and expensive. It was to be an arduous task.

None of the work on the mountain was done quickly. Francis was fortunate to have Silas available to work with him. He also had the assistance of the younger boys, Frank and Chester, and his young daughter, Florence, who helped with the surveying and had some interesting stories to tell. She said later:

> It took us several seasons to do it [the surveying]. He did all of it with a level. He'd look through the level, and I had a stake that had a line going both ways, and he'd tell me to move it left or right. Then he'd say "Stick," and I would say "Stuck." I'd hammer the stick in and that's the way we put the road up. We did that for about three summers.

> After they got the road all surveyed and they started to make the road, then my father had the crew of men, about thirteen at a time, and my brothers were included, and I cooked for all those men for two summers.

Florence may have exaggerated somewhat, although years later the other children verified her story. It was quite an undertaking for a girl who was not even a teenager at the time!

It is difficult to even imagine this undertaking. It was a monumental task, accomplished initially by only a man and his son. The expense involved in the land purchase and in hiring work crews finally necessitated the sale of some of the Little Spokane property. In 1909, he sold the farm acreage to John D. Porter, and the Cook family moved back to Spokane. Because of his age and the lack of funds, Laura tried to dissuade him from going ahead with this project, but as she said, "It could not be done."

The home at 618 East Wabash Avenue today. This was also the home of many of the Cook family children after they left the little Spokane area. (*Photo by Doris Woodward*)

Francis continued working on his mountain development in the summer months between snowfalls. Their address in Spokane was 618 East Wabash Avenue. There is some confusion about the house on Wabash, as well as the one next door. Their daughter, Laura Cook Gubser, and her children were living in the house. Her first husband, Austin Gubser, had owned it until his death in 1907. On November 24, 1909, Francis and Laura bought the house at 618 East Wabash. Daughter Laura may have owned the house next door at 614 East Wabash as well, because for the next ten years, members of the family are found at one or the other address in the Spokane city directories. After 1916, Francis and his wife lived in the house at 614 East Wabash.

During the winter months, Francis was not idle. According to wife Laura, he also joined the Spokane Chamber of Commerce and advertised his mountain project to

Spokane's leading citizens. As the road continued upwards, the Chamber of Commerce members talked about it to their friends, and in this way the mountain became known about town. People were beginning to realize the potential in Francis Cook's latest enterprise.

Christening Mount Spokane

Mount Carlton had long been called "Old Baldy," but Francis Cook felt neither name was appropriate for his beautiful mountain. He was convinced it should bear the name of the city by the falls. Others agreed with him, and it was decided to set aside a day to bestow the new name on it. On August 23, 1912, an impressive group, including Washington State Governor Marion Hay, Spokane Mayor W. J. Hindley, and Miss Spokane Marguerite Motie, gathered at the Davenport Hotel and proceeded by automobile to a spot near the summit. From there they walked or rode horses to the top. It was a gala occasion, with an impressive ceremony and the American flag waving in the breeze.

A group of dignitaries, including Gov. Marion Hay, in front of the Review Building on Riverside for a trip to the summit of Mount Spokane for its dedication. *(Photo from the "Miss Spokane" Marguerite Motie collection, courtesy Tony and Suzanne Bamonte)*

From that day forward, "Old Baldy" has been known as "Mount Spokane." The view they enjoyed that day is still available to everyone. Depending on the weather, of course, it is a 360-degree view of the Inland Northwest: to the south, the fields and undulating land of the Palouse; to the west, the Big Bend country and the town of Davenport; to the north, the Selkirks of Canada; and to the east, the lakes of northern Idaho. Twenty-six lakes and sixteen communities can be seen from various spots on the summit of Mount Spokane.

This is a spot near the summit where the motorcade ended. Francis Cook is in the background, third from the right, holding the flag. Gov. Hay is seated in the car behind the driver. *(Photo from the "Miss Spokane" Marguerite Motie collection, courtesy Tony and Suzanne Bamonte)*

The group making the final journey to the summit for the dedication ceremony of Mount Spokane. Francis Cook is fifth from the right. *(Photo from the "Miss Spokane" Marguerite Motie collection, courtesy Tony and Suzanne Bamonte)*

The group of dignitaries gathered at the site in front of the Spokane flag, which is blue, white and gold in color. Francis Cook is the tenth from the left. *(Photo from the "Miss Spokane" Marguerite Motie collection, courtesy Tony and Suzanne Bamonte)*

Raising of the flag by Gov. Hay and "Miss Spokane" Marguerite Motie. *(Photo from the Marguerite Motie collection, courtesy Tony and Suzanne Bamonte)*

Spokane Mayor W. J. Hindley, Marguerite Motie, Francis Cook and Gov. Marion Hay. *(Photo from the "Miss Spokane" Marguerite Motie collection, courtesy Tony and Suzanne Bamonte)*

A final prayer for the dedication. *(Photo from the "Miss Spokane" Marguerite Motie collection, courtesy Tony and Suzanne Bamonte)*

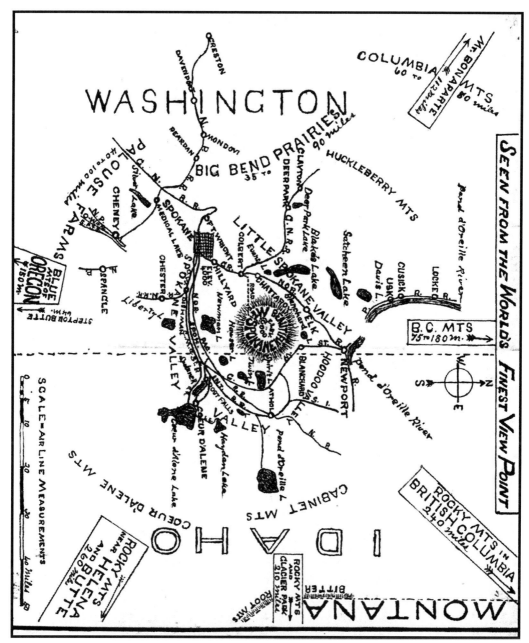

A copy of an original map drawn of Mount Spokane. Mr. Cook had put pipes on posts in concrete that pointed to the various lakes that could be seen from the top of the mountaintop. *(Drawing courtesy Cook family)*

It was a momentous occasion for Francis and justification for his determination and vision. He and some of his children continued working on the road. At some time during those years, they built two cabins, one for their own use and the other for storing equipment. Francis's wife, Laura, said "the cabin" was built in 1913. The children's accounts vary about the cabins. Clara said he never "lived" in the cabin, but she may have meant he didn't live there as a permanent home. Further research concludes he stayed there at least part of the time during the summer months.

On one thing the accounts all agree: their mother did not like the Mount Spokane project and rarely went up there with Francis. It left her alone much of the time, and she felt it was far too strenuous for Francis's health. Some of the children also resented it, because it kept their father away from home for long periods of time. This does appear to verify the story that Francis stayed in one of the cabins on the mountain at least part of the time.

The Spokane city directories provide some interesting data about Francis Cook during the years when he was working on the mountain in the summer. In 1910, he is listed as an "inventor." In 1911, he is found as the president of the Spokane Northern Electric Company. Son Silas, also living at 618 East Wabash, is called the treasurer. In 1912, Francis and Silas were the proprietors of the Hamilton Street Feed and Fuel Company. In 1914, Francis was in "real estate," and his address given as 1711 West Lidgerwood. This is the only mention of this address as a residence for the Cooks. Of interest, however, their daughter Edith is also listed in 1914 at the same address. In 1916, Francis is listed as a "promoter." From then on, he and Laura are found at 614 East Wabash, with no occupation. The directory of 1920 no longer contains the names of Francis and Laura Cook.

The Final Days

What is especially significant in this story, however, is how proud his family was of his efforts. His last child and youngest son, Ralph, wrote this description of his father:

> Father was an idealist in everything he did, it didn't make any difference if it was just a little piece of road or a road that would go for 30 miles right up Mount Spokane — it had to stay on a certain grade. ... He was fifty years ahead of people. He could see that far ahead. When I was just a boy down there at the lake, he told me: "The people will have a hard time to remember the things that are happening at this time." I remember him telling me that, and he said, "Remember different things as you can because they might be interesting later in life."

In the *Spokane Daily Chronicle* January 14, 1933, Silas Cook was eloquent in his description of his father:

When I think of my father Francis Henry Cook, and the building of the road up Mount Spokane, I think of windswept trees at timberline that have struggled onward and upward through storm-tossed elements finally reaching the heights. My father was like that—the more difficult the undertaking, the harder he fought. He never cut a tree unless it was in the way of the road.

He was a man of outstanding vision and broad sympathy. Looking out from the top of the mountain, he saw the Rockies, the Cascades, the Selkirks, and a vast panorama of hills and lake country. Looking into his inmost soul, he saw the power of the Columbia, irrigation of arid lands, native wealth unbelievable, and Spokane an inland metropolis with the world atop his mountain. My father's prophecy that Mount Spokane would become a winter and a summer playground is rapidly being fulfilled.

Shortly before my father's passing, he desired to visit the mountain that he might, as he put it, be "closer to his Maker." Like the prophets of old, he went to the mountain to pray. But he could not reach the summit [that day]. He wandered over to Skyline spring and I left him alone.

One month after he sold the Mount Spokane property, Francis Cook died on June 29, 1920, age 69, at the home he and Laura shared on Wabash Avenue. He had suffered from cancer for the last four years of his life and, although he fiercely fought it to the end, he finally lost his last battle. The funeral was held at the First Presbyterian Church, of which he and Laura were charter members. Burial was at Riverside Memorial Park. The newspapers were kind to Francis Cook and several articles were devoted to his accomplishments, although with some inaccuracies. A final tribute was paid to him by one-time foe, James N. Glover, who said, "Francis Cook was always a man of his word, straightforward, honest and independent, and a wonderfully progressive man. It was a pleasure to have helped him in some of his early enterprises in which he met with no little difficulty in carrying out." It was a nice compliment from Mr. Glover, but he apparently couldn't resist getting in his last word about the early days.

Laura Cook lived for another twenty years after her husband's death, most of the time with one or another of her children. She died August 31, 1941, and is buried with her husband at Riverside Memorial Park. She was loved by her family and highly respected by the community. Francis and Laura's years together had never been dull—they were filled with the boundless energy and imagination of this re-markable man. Now they were over for good.

Francis Cook was a man who always faced adversity head-on. Misfortune never got him down for long—he was always ready for the next challenge. This was an admirable trait. On the other hand, there was something about Francis Cook that made his frequent changes in occupation exciting for him. It was his nature. He was always making plans for the next project, so that having to move on to something different was not negative. It was just a new bridge to cross.

It must have often been difficult for his wife and family, but he could not have lived his life any other way. Going through the old records and city directories, we find the following occupations for Francis Cook: printer, editor, publisher, legislator, farmer, developer, builder, city railway executive, inventor, lawyer, surveyor, road builder and, in his final years, business owner, realtor and, finally, promoter. As his children often put it: "He always had so many irons in the fire."

This was the quintessential Francis Cook, a true, one-of-a-kind individual.

Afterword

Laura McCarty Cook

While this has primarily been an account of the accomplishments of Francis H. Cook, assuredly interesting and long-overdue, your author would like to add her opinion that much of Francis Cook's success was thanks to his wife Laura. She was a woman who not only loved her husband, but also supported him through all of his enterprises, and she did it with grace and aplomb—not to overlook the fact she was pregnant much of the time. Her well-written, non-biased accounts of their life together, published long after his death, are an invaluable resource for historians and a tribute to Laura. To me, Laura Cook is equally as heroic as her husband in this story, and my admiration for her is boundless.

Laura McCarty Cook in 1930.

(Photo courtesy Cook family)

70

Appendix I
Family History

To better understand Francis Cook and his wife, Laura, it is enlightening to investigate their ancestry. Many early members of both families exhibited the same intelligence and drive that were typical of Francis and Laura Cook. There were exceptional ancestors on both sides. All of them have stories that deserve to be recognized and honored.

The Early Cook Family

JOHNSON COOK
Francis Cook's Great-grandfather

Francis Cook's father, Silas Cook, was the grandson of a Revolutionary War soldier, Sgt. Johnson Cook, who was born in Connecticut about 1760. Neither his birth date nor his parents' names have been found to date. He enlisted in the Continental Army when he was about seventeen years of age. His enlistment papers state he was from Wallingford, Connecticut, but the records of that town do not provide a birth date for him. What is important to our story is that this young man entered the Army to join the fight against the British Redcoats and did an exemplary job.

Johnson served over six years and was discharged with the rank of sergeant on June 15, 1783, from West Point, New York. He was wounded several times in various battles and received a Badge of Honor for extraordinary conduct and courage. He returned to Wolcott, Connecticut, where he married a girl named Mary. Sadly, neither her last name nor the marriage record has so far been found.

Johnson Sr. and Mary moved to Rutland, Vermont, where the 1790 census shows they had one son under sixteen years of age and two daughters. The son was Johnson T. Cook. In 1796, they made another move—this time to Ohio. This family was only one of the vast number of Americans who participated in the huge migration from the eastern United States in the early 19th century. One of the best-known routes went west from New England, moving down the Ohio River and settling in the lands developed by the Ohio Company. Land was abundant, and possibilities were seemingly unlimited.

Marietta, in Washington County, was often a favored destination. It became the home for three generations of the Cook family, and was the birthplace of Francis H. Cook.

FORT HARMAR and MARIETTA, OHIO

Marietta and Washington County were of tremendous importance to the growth of the central United States, as this was the beginning area of much of the development westward, through Ohio and into Kentucky, Indiana, Illinois and Iowa. As an area of early 19th century settlement and development, it was unequaled.

Located at the junction of the Ohio and Muskingum rivers (directly across from western Virginia), Fort Harmar was originally built in 1785 and named in honor of Colonel Josiah Harmar, an officer in the Revolutionary War. The fort's initial purpose was to discourage illegal settlers (or squatters) from moving into the area, but the Ohio country was a huge attraction to post-Revolutionary War Americans, who were looking for good land and a better life. The area developed quickly, and settlers felt they could flee to the stockade for safety in the case of Native American attacks.

Marietta from Harmar Hill, early 1800s.
(Photo courtesy Ohio Historical Society)

The town of Marietta was settled on April 7, 1788, by 48 settlers who came from the New England states, via the Monongahela and Ohio rivers. A year before, Congress had sent another Revolutionary War veteran, Captain John Dodge, to Fort Harmar to escort to Philadelphia the chiefs of all the Indian tribes who might resist the contemplated settlement. A treaty was signed, ensuring and guaranteeing safe passage and safe settlement at the mouth of the Muskingum River. Obviously, the land of southeastern Ohio in 1788 was not an undiscovered country. Many factions foresaw the topographical advantages of this beautiful region.

Marietta was incorporated in the year 1800. What is now West Marietta was formerly Harmar. The two areas are divided by the Muskingum River and for many years were accessible to each other only by ferry. With the advent of the railroads, there was soon a railroad bridge crossing the river. The area grew continuously throughout the 19th century. Very important to the economy were boat building and machine shops, with their attendant industries.

Johnson and Mary Cook in Ohio

Johnson Cook Sr. made his living in Ohio from farming and carpentry. He received land under a Bounty Land Warrant, BLWt 5572. He also was involved in several land transactions in Marietta and in Watertown, both in Washington County. However, he is not included on the "1812 List of Ohio Taxpayers," where one would expect to find him. In his Revolutionary War Pension File S42141, a declaration by his wife, Mary, in December 1816 stated that for the past twenty-one years her husband had lived in Marietta and Adams, Washington County, Ohio. An 1820 petition from Fairfield County, Ohio, to the Pension Office includes, in addition to an inventory of his belongings, the following list of children still living at home: Mary, 30, Rachel, 21, Thomas Jefferson, 18, Elisha, 16, Meriah, 14, and Justice, 11. Wife Mary died December 18, 1844, at age 60, and was buried in the Methodist Protestant Cemetery in New Salem, Walnut Township, Fairfield County.

In the 1840 U.S. Census, Johnson Sr. and Mary were living in Perry Township. By September 1848, he had moved to Amanda Township, Fairfield County (after the death of his wife), where he died in 1848 at the age of 88. A portion of his obituary follows (the original obituary includes several battles in which Johnson did not participate—these have not been included):

DEPARTURE OF AN OLD PATRIOT

JOHNSON COOK, a Soldier of the Revolution, who was born in Connecticut in 1760, and entered the American army soon after the breaking out of the Revolution, died in Lancaster on Sunday morning, last, in the 88th year of his age.

He remained in the army six years and four months; engaged in most of the hard-fought battles … and bore with him to the grave the scars of ten wounds received in the service.

In 1796 he emigrated to Ohio, and first settled at Marietta, where he engaged in the business of a house-carpenter, and was highly useful to the new colony. His remains were followed to the grave on Monday by a large concourse of citizens and military and buried with the honors of war.

JOHNSON T. COOK
Francis Cook's Grandfather

Johnson T. Cook, the son of Johnson Sr., was the father of Silas Cook and the grandfather of Francis H. Cook. He was born in Vermont between 1780 and 1787 (accounts vary). He came to Ohio with his parents, and on May 18, 1814, married Mary Maxson, the daughter of Richard and Mary (Wells) Maxson. According to the *History of Washington Co., Ohio*: "Richard Maxon, wife and several children were residents of Marietta at 'the Point' in or near Fort Harmar during the war or part of the period of the war." Family tradition claims that Mary was born in the stockades during the time the area was being settled. Richard Maxon is later found at Fearing, Washington County, a town adjoining Marietta to the north. (The spellings Maxson and Maxon are both found in the records.)

By 1820, the younger Johnson Cook had moved his family from Marietta to Urbana, Champaign County, about 180 miles west in Ohio. He operated a "carding and fulling" factory in Urbana. In the 1820 U.S. Census of Urbana, Johnson T. Cook is listed as "J. P. Cook," with two males under 10, 1 male 16-25, 1 male 16-45 and 1 female 16-45. The 16-25-year-old male in the household may have been a brother or a laborer, but was certainly not a son. Although they purchased land in Urbana, by 1828 the family moved back to Marietta, where they are found in the 1830 census.

Listed in the 1830 U.S. Census (as Johnson P. Cook), he and Mary now had five boys and, by 1840, the four younger boys were still with them. In 1840, there is an unidentified female in the family, age 20-30. She may have been a servant, as the couple apparently had no daughters.

Their five sons were as follows:

1) Hiram, b. Ohio about 1815, m. Jane_Meserve; moved to Carter Co., Kentucky, before 1850, where he was a miller. By 1860, the family had moved to Pettis Township, Adair County, Missouri, where he was a day laborer.
2) William, b. 1817-1820; no other information has been found to date.
3) Wesley, b. Marietta on August 12, 1822; m. Delinda Wolcott. Wesley was a farmer. He served as a major in the 22nd Regiment, Kentucky Volunteer Infantry, Union Army, during the Civil War.
4) Silas, b. Urbana, Cincinnati County, Ohio, about 1825; more information follows.
5) Edwin, b. Urbana on January 24, 1828; m. Julia Downs, farmer. They moved to Grayson Co., Kentucky, before 1860, and father Johnson T. Cook, gardener, lived with them. They were at that time living next door to Edwin's brother Wesley and his family. Edwin served in the same regiment as Wesley during the Civil War and attained the rank of captain.

The above family has been constructed from several sources, family records and censuses. There is corroboration of the strong ties between these families, as they are found living next door to each other at various times. There is also an important document dated September 21, 1845, which provides proof of the relationships. It gives details of a loan of $100, which Johnson T. Cook made to son Silas. The document refers to "Wesley Cook, a brother to Silas." There is a also a diary, written by Elias Wolcott, Wesley Cook's father-in-law, in which he mentions Silas, Wesley, Edwin and "Father and Mother Cook" several times.

By 1870, Wesley and Edwin, with their families, moved to Cincinnati Township, Harrison County, Iowa. Their father, Johnson, accompanied them there and died in Harrison County on April 26, 1868, at age 88.

SILAS COOK
Francis Cook's Father

Silas Cook, the fourth son of Johnson T. and Mary (Maxson) Cook, is the person of greatest interest to this story. He and his wife were the parents of several exceptional children, not the least of whom was Francis H. Cook. Laura Cook, Francis's wife, recalled many years later that her father-in-law "was a man of integrity, companionable to his seven boys as well as with his neighbors." Silas Cook was also a man of intelligence and ability, traits he passed along to his children.

Silas Cook was born in 1825 in Urbana, Champaign County, Ohio. Within five years, the Johnson T. Cook family had migrated back to Marietta and, on November 24, 1846, Silas married Catharine Wheeler Ford. The couple lived on the western side of the Muskingum River in Harmar (now West Marietta). At the time of the 1850 U.S. Census, they had two children: Frederick, born 1848, and Lucian, born 1849. Silas is listed as an engineer.

Silas Cook
(Photo courtesy Cook family)

By the 1860 census, they had the following children, who were originally listed only by their initials:

1) Frederick J., age 13
2) Lucian Ford, age 11
3) Franklin Pierce, a twin, age 9
4) Francis Henry, a twin, age 9. It is not known which twin was born first.
5) Joseph Silas, age 4
6) Mary Lavina, female, age 2
7) Charles Augustus, age 5/12

Family records say there was another girl, Harriet C., born to Silas and Catherine in 1856, who died before the 1860 census was taken.

CATHARINE WHEELER FORD
Francis Cook's Mother

Catharine was born on March 2, 1828, in Watertown Township, Washington County, Ohio, the second child born to Joseph North Ford and Clarissa Wheeler. (A first daughter, Elizabeth, was born in 1825 and died in 1828.) Hers is an interesting ancestry. Joseph North Ford was born about 1801 in Ohio and, according to Ohio records, married Clarissa Wheeler on December 15, 1824. Clarissa was the daughter of Samuel Wheeler and Julia Odell, who were married on January 22, 1792, in Stratford, Connecticut. Her father, Samuel Wheeler, was a Revolutionary War soldier, having served in the Connecticut State Guard for twelve months under John Odell, after which he reenlisted in 1781 for another year. The last eight months of his service were spent as a corporal in the Connecticut Line.

Catharine went to school in Washington County, Ohio. Her middle name "Wheeler" was given to her in honor of her ancestor, and she later became an early member of the Daughters of the American Revolution shortly after it was founded in 1890. Catharine had four siblings:

1) Giles, born August 23, 1830
2) Henry, born October 21, 1832
3) Lavina, born August 2, 1833
4) Augustus, born December 25, 1839

All of her brothers must have been important to Catharine and her husband, as their names were perpetuated in the Cook families to come.

The Move To Iowa

In 1863, Silas and his family moved to Iowa, a journey described in Section I of this book. The Cooks remained in Iowa for thirteen years, living first in Council Bluffs. By the 1870 census, they had moved to Magnolia in Harrison County, just north of Pottawattamie County. Silas is listed as a farmer. By then, son Francis had left the fold, and their little daughter, Mary, had died. Fred was a clerk in the treasurer's office, Lucian was a dry goods clerk, Frank was a dry goods merchant, Joseph was at school and Charles and his recently born brother, Giles Hildreth Cook, were at home. Francis is found as a student at the State University of Iowa in Iowa City.

Farming was apparently not Silas's major interest in life. Having been called an engineer in earlier censuses, it is found in later years he definitely had engineering ability and was involved in several inventions related particularly to railroading, including an air brake, the Penberthy injector, and an automatic boiler feeder, for

S. COOK.
Automatic Boiler-Feeders.

No. 5,276.   Reissued Feb. 11, 1873.

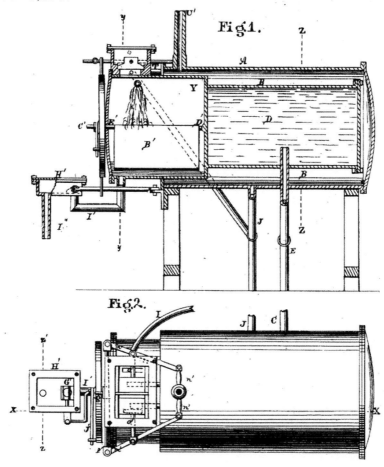

Fig.1.

Fig.2.

Attest.
C. J. Hale
Jeremiah Furbig.

Silas Cook, Ass. to
Automatic Boiler Feeder Co.
per Fisher + Fisher
Attys.

Inventor.

(From the United States Patent Office)

77

S. COOK.
Automatic Boiler-Feeders.

No. 5,276.

Reissued Feb. 11, 1873.

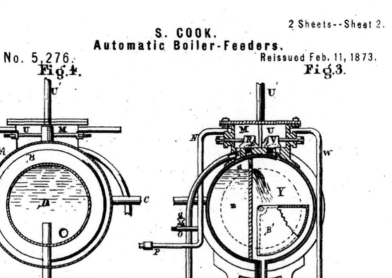

Fig.4.

Fig.3.

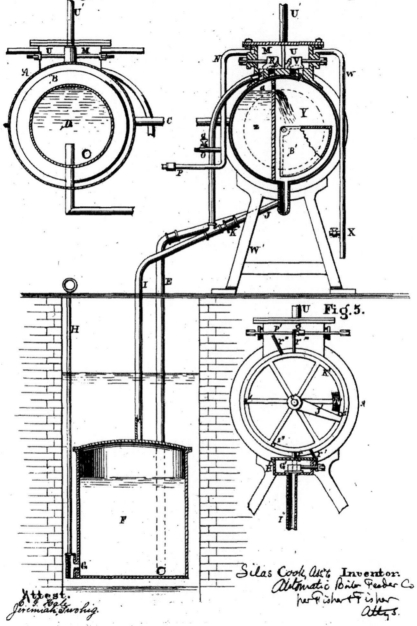

Fig.5.

Silas Cook Ass't Inventor.
Automatic Boiler Feeder Co
per Fisher & Fisher
Att'ys.

Attest.
Jeremiah Twohig.

78

which he received Patent No. 5,276 on February 11, 1873, as the inventor. He was either employed by or connected with the Automatic Boiler Feeder Company at the time the patent was issued. His inventive abilities were inherited by at least two of his sons, Lucian and Francis.

The Move to Tacoma

In 1877, Silas and Catharine left their home in Iowa and, with sons Charles and Giles, joined Francis in Western Washington. They came to Puget Sound from Omaha via railroad to Sacramento. From there they took a one-hundred-mile steamship ride down the Sacramento River to San Francisco, an ocean trip out through the Golden Gate to Portland, a forty-mile Columbia River ride to Kalama, and finally a one-hundred-mile trip on the Northern Pacific Railroad, reaching Tacoma, the "City of Destiny," in October 1877. It was a joyous family reunion when they joined their son Francis.

Silas and Catharine later built a home adjoining the Chamber of Commerce building in New Tacoma and, according to Catharine's obituary, the Cooks were important for the rest of their lives in the industrial, educational and

Silas Cook home in New Tacoma.
(Photo courtesy Cook family)

religious history of Tacoma. Still called a farmer, Silas owned property on Vashon Island, which he farmed and brought the produce to Tacoma to sell.

According to the 1880 Territorial Census of New Tacoma, Silas Cook was a supervisor of roads, and son Charles was working as a printer. Giles, age eleven, is called a "daughter," obviously a mistake made by the census taker. Silas died in Tacoma in 1885 and is buried there at Oakwood Cemetery.

Catharine Cook's obituary in the *Tacoma Daily News* states that she died on January 24, 1910, just one week after the death of her son Lucian. Catharine was highly respected in the Tacoma area and was known as "Grandma Cook" by her many friends. In her later years she was able to make several visits to her childhood home in Marietta, Ohio. Besides being a member of the DAR, she was a long-

Catharine Cook
(Photo courtesy Cook family)

time member of the First Congregational Church in Tacoma. She was buried beside her husband at Oakwood Cemetery. Her finest testimonial comes from her daughter-in-law, Laura Cook, who wrote: "Francis's mother, who lived to be 82, made as fine a mother-in-law as one could wish. She was a Christian woman of keen intellect, devoted to her family and to her church, admired and beloved by all." Her obituary also gives a brief glimpse of her sons, all of whom with the exception of Frederick, attended her funeral. She and Silas were both special individuals and passed on their best attributes to Francis and the other Cook boys.

FRANCIS COOK'S BROTHERS

Several of the older Cook sons did not migrate to the Washington coast with their parents. Some of them came at a later time, but meanwhile they were building lives for themselves in Iowa, Nebraska and Kansas.

Frederick J. Cook

Frederick J. Cook married a Missouri girl, Ella Duncan, and in 1880 they were living with their one-year-old daughter, Olive, in Severance, Doniphan County, Kansas, where Frederick was a lumber merchant. The following year, they had another daughter, Katherine. In 1889, Frederick and his family moved to Pierce County, Washington, where he dealt in real estate. Another daughter, Elsie, was born at this time. By 1910, they were back in Missouri, living in St. Joseph with daughter, Elsie. Frederick was a bookkeeper at this time. Before 1920, they moved to Kansas City, Missouri, where Frederick died on February 24, 1920.

Lucian Ford Cook

On November 10, 1873, Lucian Ford Cook married a Massachusetts girl named Cora Manning. The couple later moved to Dunlap in Harrison County, Missouri, with a daughter, Kate, and son, Clarence. Lucian published the *Dunlap Reporter* from 1873 until 1881. It was the fourth newspaper in Harrison County. Within a few years, he was in Pierce County near his parents.

Lucian Cook moved to Tacoma about 1884-1885. He was a man of exceptional ability. He was not only active in real estate but also invented a plan for an elevated railway. He built a small, working model of the railway from Central Street in Tacoma to Spanaway, but the Panic of 1893 put an end to the project. He later became a keen advocate of the small boats and steamers on Puget Sound, which he called the "Mosquito Fleet." He owned several of these small and lively boats himself, taking a personal interest in the welfare of the whole fleet. He soon earned the title of "Commodore." His efforts on behalf of these boats, which he considered a vital part of Tacoma's industry and growth, are very reminiscent of Francis Cook's eager involvement in many noteworthy public projects. Lucian was an extraordinary and innovative man. He and his wife, Cora, had four sons and three daughters. He died in Tacoma on January 17, 1910, shortly before his mother.

Franklin Pierce Cook

Franklin P. Cook, Francis H. Cook's twin brother, married Emma Berkey, a girl from Pennsylvania, on October 3, 1871, in Magnolia, Iowa. While in Iowa, Franklin and Emma's two children were born: a daughter, Mary Bruce, born January 22, 1874, and a son, Norman Bruce, born August 4, 1875. In 1880, the family was living in Oakland, Burt County, Nebraska, just west of Omaha in the same neighborhood as his cousin Wesley J. Cook, a son of Silas Cook's brother, Edwin. Franklin was a lumber dealer.

Sometime after 1880, possibly at the same time his older brother Lucian moved to Tacoma, Franklin and his family moved to Pierce County, Washington, near his parents and his twin brother. There Franklin worked as a brick dealer. By the late 1880s, he and his family moved to Spokane at the urging of his twin brother, Francis. More about Frank's life can be found in Section II of this book.

Joseph Silas Cook

Joseph Silas Cook, the fourth son, was a railroad conductor in Missouri Valley, Harrison County, Iowa, when the census was taken, and was a boarder in a large rooming house. On September 20, 1881, in Harrison County, Iowa, he married Sarah (Sallie) Berkley of Ohio. They also would eventually live in Pierce County.

Sallie Berkley Cook
(Photo courtesy Cook family)

Very little is known about this fifth son of Silas and Catharine. He may have come to the Tacoma area with his older brother Lucian or with Franklin, but there is no record of it. Joseph and Sallie had no children. Joseph was a railroad conductor, and in 1910, he and Sallie were living next door to his brother Charles and his family. Joseph died in January 1928 at Tacoma; Sallie died there in July 1938.

Joseph S. Cook
(Photo courtesy Cook family)

Charles Augustus Cook

Charles Cook was highly respected as one of Tacoma's prominent pioneers. On July 25, 1882, he married Sarah Dellafield
"Della" Charnock, the daughter of Mr. and Mrs. William
Charnock, emigrants from England. The *Tacoma Sunday
Ledger* of July 24, 1932, published a complimentary article about Charles and Della who, according to the *Ledger*, were celebrating their 50th anniversary. Charles began his life in Tacoma as a printer, working for his brother
Francis, but later quit the printing business and made his
money in real estate booms, both in the Tacoma area and
on Vashon and Maury islands. He platted some of Vashon
Island, where he named a portion of shoreline property
"Magnolia Beach," in honor of his boyhood home in Iowa.

Charles A. Cook
(Photo courtesy Cook family)

Charles served as Pierce County assessor in 1913 and 1914
and was always active in civic affairs in Tacoma. He was
the editor of the first literary society in February 1878, of
which brother Francis served as critic. Charles and Della were longtime members of the First Congregational
Church, where Charles sang tenor in the church choir,
the only mention of musical ability on the Cook side
of the family. Many years later, in 1944, Charles wrote
an account of his early years. Much of the information
known about the Cooks' journey from Marietta to Iowa
and later to Tacoma has come from the pen of this man, an
excellent writer. At the time, he and brother Giles were the
last living sons of Silas and Catharine Cook. He later returned to Marietta, Ohio, in hopes of finding some trace of
the early Cook family that might still be living in the area. He returned to Tacoma
via Nebraska and Southern California, where he visited his son Burton.

Della Charnock Cook
(Photo courtesy Cook family)

Charles and Della had three children: Ethel, Arthur A. and Burton A. Their son
Arthur later moved to Spokane, where he was a bridge inspector for a railroad; and
Burton first moved to Seattle and later lived in Southern California. Charles died in
Tacoma on April 23, 1945.

Giles Hildreth Cook

Giles Cook, the youngest of the Cook boys, married Emmalena Johnson of Philadelphia on November 19, 1890, in Tacoma. They moved to Snohomish, where they
remained for the rest of their lives. He was the owner/operator of the Bruhn &

82

Giles H. Cook
(Photo courtesy Cook family)

Henry grocery store, which he owned until 1949.

He was the last surviving charter member of the United Commercial Travelers. Giles Cook died March 9, 1950, and his wife died nine days later, on March 18th. The couple had one son, Jack Cook, and three daughters: Ruth Cook Eagle, Lois Cook Henning, and Marjorie Cook Sherman.

Emmalena Cook
(Photo courtesy Cook family)

THE KINCAID and McCARTY FAMILIES
Wagon Trains West

The William Moore Kincaid Family

Laura McCarty's mother, Ruth Jane Kincaid McCarty, was the oldest child of William Kincaid and Nancy Woolery of Missouri. Both the Kincaid and Woolery families had settled in Kentucky after the Revolutionary War, and several members of both families later migrated to Missouri, where William and Nancy were married on February 11, 1836, in Marion County. By 1850, Nancy Kincaid had borne the following seven children, all born in Missouri:

1) Ruth Jane, born December 8, 1836
2) John Francis, born December 6, 1838
3) Susanna, born March 3, 1840
4) William Christopher, born December 1842
5) James F., born January 1844
6) Laura F., born August 3, 1846
7) Joseph Cooper, born October 1, 1849

The entire Kincaid family is found in the 1850 U.S. Census, but shortly after the census was taken, Nancy Kincaid died on December 22, 1850, and her widower husband, William, decided to take his seven mother-

William Moore Kincaid
(Photo courtesy Cook family)

less children to the West. His oldest child Ruth, then sixteen years of age, took care of the younger children, aged two to fourteen, during the long journey.

In 1853, when William Kincaid left Missouri for the West, his family was part of a 52-wagon train to the Pacific Northwest. Along with the Kincaid family in the wagon train were Abraham, Isaac and James Woolery, brothers of William Kincaid's deceased wife, Nancy, as well as Julia and James McCullough. Julia McCullough was Nancy Kincaid's sister. James Woolery died of consumption near Yakima in 1853. The train went over the Cascade Mountains on the old Naches Trail, noted as being one of the most difficult passages to the Pacific Coast. They were the first wagon train to use the "road." The descent on the west side was so steep the pioneers sometimes had to get out of the wagons and lower them over the cliffs by ropes. Their amazing feat in getting through these difficulties has been memorialized by a Naches Trail Marker, which honors the members of the party.

The Jonathan McCarty Family

Laura McCarty's father, Jonathan Warren McCarty, was born on May 20, 1833, in La Porte, Indiana, the son of Benjamin and Deida (Walker) McCarty. By the 1850 census, his mother was deceased, and the family was living in Cedar Creek Township, Lake County, Indiana, where Benjamin was the assistant marshal and signed the Lake County census that year.

THE NACHES TRAIL

The Naches Pass Trail had a long history of human use by the time the Kincaid family crossed it. It was a route used by early Native Americans to get across the Cascades, and Hudson's Bay employees had been crossing at that point by the mid-1830s. Later, George McClellan, who had been President Lincoln's moody and testy first general of the Army of the Potomac during the Civil War, surveyed the pass as a possible railroad route and pronounced it unfavorable for that purpose. In fact, he believed the Cascades were inaccessible by railroad, although he later conceded Snoqualmie Pass or nearby Stampede Pass might be a possibility. The Northern Pacific Railroad eventually followed that course, many years later.

Naches Trail Marker

In the early years of the western migration, Naches Pass became known as the "Walla Walla to Steilacoom Citizen Trail." Today it is known as the route of the Longmire or the "Longmire/Biles Wagon Train." Both names are commemorated on the monument, as are the names "Kincaid" and "Woolery."

Early in 1850, a wagon train was being planned in Lake County to make the journey west. Jonathan Mc-Carty and his brothers, Lafayette and Morgan, were definitely interested. The organizer of the train was George Belshaw Jr., of West Creek Township, adjoining Cedar Creek. George Jr. was the husband of Candace McCarty, the sister of Jonathan and his brothers. The train eventually consisted of ten wagons and twenty-five persons, including the McCarty boys and George Belshaw's parents, George Sr. and Elizabeth (Archer) Belshaw. The train left Lake County in May 1853. By the time it crossed the Mississippi River, they had elected George Belshaw Jr. as captain of the train, and it was known thereafter as the "Belshaw Train."

Jonathan W. McCarty
(Photo courtesy Cook family)

They arrived in Eugene, Oregon, in October 1853. Jonathan did not remain there for very long, as he is found soon after in the Puyallup area of Western Washington.

Early Years in Puyallup

On January 1, 1854, after getting across the mountains, Kincaid and his eldest son, John, made their way down to Fort Steilacoom on the Stuck River and took up a donation land claim of 160 acres in the Puyallup Valley on the site of the present town of Sumner. The Woolerys also settled in the Sumner/Puyallup area. Those coming after William Kincaid used his claim corners as the starting point for their own claims. According to the *Daffodil Valley Times*, William Kincaid is considered Sumner, Washington's first settler. He was well known in the area as a man of fine character.

Jonathan McCarty arrived in the Puyallup Valley not long after the Kincaids and took up a claim on the Stuck River directly across from the Kincaids. Jonathan and Ruth Kincaid soon met and fell in love. They were married on February 12, 1855. As there was no minister in the Puyallup Valley at that time, they sent to Steilacoom for Justice of the Peace Sherwood Bonney. However, Bonney was not authorized to perform marriages in King County, so the couple and the justice of the peace took a boat and rowed across the river to Pierce County. This was the first marriage performed in the Puyallup Valley.

Ruth Kincaid McCarty
(Photo courtesy Cook family)

Soon after their marriage, the settlers in the valley were warned that marauding Indians were coming to

THE BELSHAW WAGON TRAIN
and Marshall Belshaw Shore

So much has been written about the Kincaid family and their journey west that the story of Jonathan McCarty and the Belshaw wagon train has virtually been lost in the family records. Thanks to Marshall Shore, the Belshaw journey has been preserved and another aspect of the Kincaid/McCarty/Cook family can be added to the family history. This story of the Belshaw wagon train was his legacy to his ancestors and to their descendants.

Marshall Shore
(From the Shore collection)

The journey west made by the Belshaw wagon train has been preserved in two diaries—one kept by George Belshaw Sr. and the other by his sister-in-law, Sarah (Parsons) Belshaw. The diaries provide a day-by-day account of the tedious journey, sometimes pleasant, sometimes sad. Sarah in particular often refers to the home she left behind in Indiana. George's account is a more matter-of-fact description of the trip. This Godly group never traveled on the Sabbath but used the time to rest themselves and their animals and to praise God. Both writers frequently mention the graves and the dead animals along the route that were constant reminders of the dangers around them.

Preserving the diaries is the result of the research and dedication of a Belshaw/McCarty descendant, Marshall Belshaw Shore, who inherited the diary of George Sr., his great-grandfather. Marshall's grandfather, Marshall Winfield Belshaw, was a one-year-old on the journey. Through the McCartys, Marshall Shore was the first cousin, twice removed, of Laura McCarty Cook. Marshall was never aware of this recently discovered fact, as he died in June 2009, but he would have been delighted to know of the connection.

As a career officer with the United States Air Force as a navigator, Marshall served in the European Theater during World War II and later in Korea. Many years later, he wrote a book about his experiences in the two conflicts. Marshall was a meticulous researcher, always interested in history and sharing his findings. After retiring from the Air Force, he moved to Spokane, Washington, and was a longtime member of the Westerners Spokane Corral, never losing his love of Western history. In recent years, he authored a book about his hometown of Farmington, Washington, where he is buried and where George and Candace Belshaw's son, Marshall Winfield Belshaw, homesteaded after leaving Eugene, Oregon. [Editor's note: Doris Woodward, the author of this publication, was the editor and assisted Mr. Shore in writing the book about Farmington.]

the area, and the families fled to Steilacoom for safety. When they returned, they found their homes had been destroyed and their stock carried away. In hopes of finding some kind of employment, Jonathan and Ruth decided to leave.

They moved to Eugene, Oregon, where their first child, Charles, was born in 1856. They stayed there until the fall of 1859, coming back to Steilacoom with ten oxen to sell. According to Jonathan, the journey was difficult, as Ruth was carrying their eighteen-month-old baby, and was also pregnant. It was a rough, hard trip, and Ruth was thrown from her horse three times, fortunately with no damage.

In February, shortly after their return to their homestead on the Stuck River, daughter Clara was born. In the ensuing years, their family grew to include six children:

1) Charles C., born March 22, 1856, in Oregon; in the 1880 census he was attending school in California. He married Mary Lewis.
2) Clara Antoinette, born February 12, 1858, in Steilacoom; in the 1880 census she was teaching school. She married John Henry Wilt.
3) Laura Candace, born March 22, 1860, in Sumner; married Francis H. Cook.
4) Mary Estelle, born March 22, 1862, in Washington Territory. She married (1) Rev. Thomas M. Boyd; married (2) Rev. L. W. Simmons.
5) William W., born in 1866 in Washington Territory.
6) Frank Truman, born September 1876 in Seattle; married Maude Jane Berlin.

In early 1870, the family moved to Seattle, because they wanted to ensure their children would be able to receive better educations. Rural schools often lacked many of the advantages of more populated areas. It should be noted, however, that the first school in Pierce County was started in 1854, so the county can pride itself on doing what it was able to do very early. Jonathan was a storekeeper in Seattle, and the older girls attended school.

It was the beginning of an outstanding career for Clara McCarty, their oldest daughter. At age 18, she entered the Territorial University, which became the University of Washington. Clara was the first graduate of the school and received a bachelor of science degree. Tuition at the time was $30.00 per year. After graduation, Clara taught at several schools and then attended the University of California. She was elected the first female Pierce County superintendent of schools in 1880. McCarty Hall, a dormitory on the present University of Washington campus, was named in her honor.

Laura McCarty did not have as prestigious career as her older sister. However, she was a student at the university and later taught school in Sumner, according to her daughter Clara. Her marriage to Francis Cook ended her school teaching years, but

Laura was throughout her life dedicated to education, particularly in the education of her daughters.

By the 1880 census, the McCartys were back in Pierce County, where Jonathan was a farmer. He and Ruth remained in Sumner, Washington, for the rest of their lives. Ruth died on September 11, 1880, and Jonathan was married again in February 1883 to Sarah Wesbrook. Both Jonathan and Ruth are buried at the Sumner Pioneer Cemetery.

Clara Antoinette McCarty   Laura Candace McCarty

(Photos courtesy Cook family)

The Later Years

All his life William Kincaid was known to be an honorable man. According to the *Daffodil Valley Times*, he shared most pioneers' dislike of Indians, but he always tried to be fair in his dealings with them. After the Indian Wars of 1855-1856, Nisqually Chief Leschi was arrested and put on trial for the murder of an American soldier, Colonel A. Benton Moses. Kincaid and his neighbor, Ezra Meeker, who both served on the jury, refused to convict the Indian leader, causing a hung jury and preventing him from being hanged, at least for the time being. A second trial was held. This time Chief Leschi was found guilty and was hanged on February 19,

1858, a gross injustice that was reversed by the Washington State Senate in 2004 in Resolution 8727, which recognized Leschi as a "courageous leader" and a "great and noble man." It was also an exoneration of William Kincaid and Ezra Meeker for their decision in the first trial. Their descendants certainly can be proud of the difficult and unpopular stand taken by these two men in the first trial.

Ezra Meeker, who was a great admirer of his friend, later wrote of William Kincaid:

> In character, in fine sensibility, in true righteousness, in upright dealings with his neighbors, in firmness to stand for what he believed to be right, he was the peer of any man I ever knew – he was pure gold.

William Kincaid died in 1870 and left behind a family and legacy of values that were important to Sumner for years to come. His daughter, Laura Kincaid, was the first schoolteacher in Washington Territory, and another daughter, Susannah, married Levant Thompson, a member of the first territorial legislature.

Thus ends the story of the Cooks, the Fords, the McCartys and the Kincaids—all people who contributed to the two individuals who are the subject of this book. Both Francis and Laura McCarty Cook were the descendants of typical American families, not especially wealthy, but immensely rich in those special America traits: honesty, ability and determination.

Appendix II
The Cook Children

Francis and Laura Cook had an impressive number of children—a total of eleven, born over a period of nineteen years. All of the children were still living when Francis Cook died in 1920, an almost unique fact in those years when infant deaths were common and few families had all of their children live to be adults.

The Cook children were raised in a loving but strict environment. Several of them were interviewed late in their lives and were all in agreement their parents were very special people. Their memories, however, were not all the same—perhaps because there was such a difference in their ages. The youngest children probably didn't even know the oldest ones very well. They grew up in different places and had different perspectives about what happened.

Learning about all of them is a fascinating look at a turn-of-the-century American family.

A BRIEF OVERVIEW

1. Katharine Ruth Cook, born November 11, 1881
2. Laura May Cook, born June 30, 1883
3. Silas Warren Cook, born April 30, 1885
4. Clara Emma Cook, born January 12, 1887
5. Frank Arthur Cook, born September 2, 1888/1889
6. Chester Robert Cook, born July 12, 1890
7. Edith Lee Cook, born February 2, 1892
8. Lolita Evelyn Cook, born November 13, 1893
9. Florence Helene Cook, born November 26, 1896
10. Winifred Josephine Cook, born November 22, 1898
11. Ralph Wheeler Cook, born October 9, 1900

Three of the Cook children—Clara, Florence and Ralph—were interviewed in later years by Louis Livingston, a Spokane man who loved history and spent many years interviewing local people and taping their oral histories. Mr. Livingston taught history and government classes at Lewis & Clark High School in Spokane from 1938 to 1966. He was later the director of the Cheney Cowles Museum, now the Museum of Arts and Culture (MAC). In 1957, he contacted John Ellingson, who frequently worked at the museum, about his oral interviews and asked John to transcribe them for him. There were more than forty in all, and it took John the better part of 1958 to do the job. Mr. Livingston insisted on reading and checking John's transcriptions.

He advised Ellingson he didn't want them to be made available to the public until after his death. John was faithful to that request.

Livingston's entire life was devoted to the betterment of Spokane through many worthy causes. He was the last living charter member of the Westerners Spokane Corral at the time of his death in 2007 at the age of 107.

John Ellingson was honored to receive the prestigious "Minuteman Award" from the National Sons of the American Revolution in 2010. He is also an active, longtime member of the Westerners Spokane Corral.

All who are interested in the Francis Cook story owe a tremendous debt of gratitude to both of these men, for preserving the accounts of three of the Cook children. The children's memories provide significant details of their lives and those of their parents.

The Francis Cook family in 1911 at 618 East Wabash. Standing, left to right: Laura Cook Gubser, Florence Cook, Emma Toombs Cook, Chester Cook, Ralph Cook (in front of Chester), Katharine Cook Alvis, Winifred Cook, Melvin Alvis, Francis Cook, Frank Cook, Laura McCarty Cook, Lolita Cook and Edith Cook. Sitting in front: Harold Gubser and Genevieve Gubser. Missing from photo are Clara and Silas Cook.
(Photo courtesy Cook family)

KATHARINE RUTH COOK
First Child

Katharine Ruth "Kate" was born in Spokane on November 11, 1881, when her parents were living in the *Spokan Times* building at Riverside and Howard. She was named after Francis's mother, Catharine Wheeler Ford, and Laura's mother, Ruth Jane Kincaid McCarty. Katharine was married January 5, 1905, in the Cook home on the Little Spokane River. Her husband was William Alvis, born February 2, 1880, in Pike County, Missouri, the son of Shadrack and Lucinda Jane Kendrick.

William and Katharine were both teachers. William was the superintendent of schools in Latah, Washington, and later was elected principal at Coulee City. He died in Rosalia of tuberculosis October 24, 1918. He and Katharine had one son, Melvin Burton Alvis, born in Spokane on June 15, 1916, always called "Burton." He married Elizabeth Ogden on July 10, 1940, in San Anselmo, Marin County, California.

William and Katharine Alvis
(Photo courtesy Cook family)

After her husband's death, Katharine lived in Yakima and continued teaching school to support herself and her son. When Francis Cook died, Katharine and Burton had the pleasure and good fortune of having her mother stay with them for several

Burton Alvis
(Photo courtesy Cook family)

years. On August 27, 1931, Katharine received her bachelor of arts degree from the University of Washington. What a fine example of determination for a 50-year-old widow with a teenage son!

Burton probably stayed with his grandmother while his mother was finishing her degree. When he was growing up, Burton was with his grandmother a lot of the time. He later said of her, "She was a gentle, kindly, encouraging person, who was always there to listen to my day's activities—the perfect grandma." It was during that time that Laura wrote her articles for the *Spokane Chronicle*.

Katharine was also a Sunday school teacher for the First Presbyterian Church in Yakima for twenty-five years. Burton said it was his mother's favorite pastime. On June 14, 1951, Katharine received a letter from the Yakima newspaper, which said, in part: "It is with some regret that we read that you were retiring from the superintending of the Presbyterian Sunday School ... it means that one who has faithfully served a number of generations of youth will no longer be active. ... Grateful thanks of not only your church but the entire community." It was a fine tribute to a woman who exhibited the best of both her parents.

Katharine Cook Alvis died in Portland on April 30, 1972. Melvin Burton Alvis became a Presbyterian minister. He later described his mother as being strict, but loving and caring. "Her best qualities were her honesty, frankness and loyalty ... and her greatest legacy was her love for God and for the church." His mother certainly influenced her son Burton's decision to become a minister. He died on April 8, 2008 in Portland, Oregon.

LAURA MAY COOK
Second Child

Laura May was born in Spokane on June 30, 1883, but her birthplace is in doubt. She was born sometime in the transition period between the sale of the *Spokan Times* and the move to the small house on the South Hill. She was named af-

ter her mother, but the name "May" appears to have no family significance. However, to her nieces and nephews, she was always known as "Auntie May."

She was married at the First Presbyterian Church in Spokane on August 7, 1902, to Austin Albert Gubser. He was born about 1872, the son of Andrew Gubser and Letitia Smith. Laura and Austin were both teachers, like her sister and brother-in-law, Katharine and William Alvis. They taught in Spokane, where he was the deputy superintendent of schools. They had two children: Genevieve Gubser, born October 31, 1903, who married Russell Huntsinger in 1933 and died January 15, 1997, in Kalispell, Flathead County, Montana; and Harold Gubser, born May 11, 1907, who married Edna Ring in 1927 and died in December 1985 in Spokane.

**Austin and Laura Gubser
with Harold and Genevieve**
(Photo courtesy Cook family)

Sadly, Austin Gubser died on August 22, 1908, leaving May with two small children. The Gubser family was living at 618 East Wabash when he died, and it was to this house that Francis and Laura Cook moved with their younger children when they left the Little Spokane property about 1909.

Laura McCarty Cook was a loving grandmother to her daughter's two babies, and there was a strong bond between the mother and daughter during that time. Laura May lived with her parents on East Wabash until 1913, when she married Francis (Frank) Alfred Stookey, who had been born in Illinois on May 20, 1881, and moved as a young boy with his parents to a farm in Wilbur, Washington. Frank Stookey served many years in Wilbur as a city marshal and a water commissioner.

Laura May and Frank had three children: Edith Loma (who went by Loma), Frank Thomas "Tom" and Robert Lee "Bob." Loma was born in June 1914 and died May 3, 1924, at the age of nine. She suffered from mastoiditis, a condition that today can be treated successfully. Tom was born April 11, 1916, and died in Seattle on May 13, 1963. He married Zelda Stebber on October 9, 1939. Bob was born on August 8, 1917, and died in Washington in July 1982. He was married to Patricia Gorman in 1942.

Laura holding Tom Stookey, Harold Gubser and Genevieve Gubser, and Frank holding Loma. *(Photo courtesy Cook family)*

Both Tom and Bob began their careers driving buses for Washington Motor Coach in the 1930s. When World War II began, Tom was unable to join any of the military services due to his severe allergies. It was a huge disappointment to him. Bob joined the Army and spent three years as an infantryman in the South Pacific, mostly fighting in New Guinea. Both Tom and Bob spent the rest of their adult careers driving for Greyhound.

In the late '40s, Frank and Laura Stookey were divorced. In 1948, Frank suffered a stroke and moved to a rest home in Spokane to be nearer his sons. He died on May 31, 1950. Laura May Stookey died May 15, 1968, in Spokane, where she was living at 1308 West 15th Avenue. Her obituary mentions she had taught school in Spokane, as well as in Wilbur and Moses Lake. Her grandson Frank Stookey recalls that she taught in several Washington cities after WWII, including Davenport. Also according to Frank, she was especially proud of her membership with the Spokane

Pioneer Association. She was also a member of the First Presbyterian Church. She was buried at Greenwood Memorial Terrace with her mother and father. May's surviving children were her daughter, Mrs. Russell Huntsinger, and her two sons, Harold Gubser and Robert Stookey.

"Auntie May" was remembered as being very soft and cuddly. She made huge hair bows, which were popular in the early 1900s, and she loved hats, which she wore whenever she went out. She was the first of the Cooks' seven daughters to die.

SILAS WARREN COOK
Third Child

Silas Warren was born April 30, 1885, and named after his paternal grandfather. He was married October 24, 1916, to Amy Morris in Coeur d'Alene, Idaho. The couple had two children, both born in Spokane: Warren Lawrence Cook, born July 29, 1925, and Charles Edward Cook, born October 21, 1927.

Silas Warren Cook
(Photo courtesy Cook family)

Contrary to his obituary and many other printed sources, Silas Cook was *not* born in the *Spokan Times* building at Riverside and Howard. The Cook family was no longer living there in 1885. This is proven by land records and newspaper accounts, all of which indicate that Francis Cook was farming on the South Hill by 1885.

Being the oldest son in the family put Silas in a different position from the other children. He was instrumental in assisting his father with the Mount Spokane project. Without him, it is doubtful whether Francis Cook would have made a success of the venture. While the younger boys were certainly a help at various times, Francis depended on his older son far more. This is a possible explanation of why Silas waited until he was thirty-one years old to get married. He was simply too busy helping his father. He apparently never had any advanced education but was successful in several endeavors during his life.

At one time, Silas went into business for himself with a sawmill, logging in the area around Newman Lake, on Peone Prairie and near Dartford, where the Cooks' Little Spokane property was located. Before he was married, he lived for a while with his parents on East Wabash. He and his father began the Spokane Northern Electric Company and later started the Hamilton Street Feed & Fuel Company.

His obituary in the April 21, 1966, issue of the *Spokesman-Review* states Silas later purchased property in what is now the Wandermere area and farmed it. He built a brick home there and did almost all of the work himself. In 1938, Silas Cook ran for county commissioner of the First District on the Republican ticket. One of his most commendable opinions as a potential candidate was his opposition to putting campaign posters on the telephone poles. Good for him!

In 1941, Silas built a roller skating rink on North Division, the present-day Pattison's. He built it of rough lumber and salvaged timber. Five years later, in 1946, he purchased a skating rink in Dishman, Washington, which he and his son Charles operated for many years. They continuously improved and enlarged it, until it was one of the largest in the country.

Amy Morris Cook
(Photo courtesy Cook family)

Silas Cook died April 20, 1966. Five years later, his wife, Amy, married Charles Jensen and moved to Waterville County, Washington. In the late 1980s, she moved to Lake Elsinore to live with her surviving son, Charles. She died there on January 17, 1989. Silas and Amy are both buried at Riverside Memorial Park in the Cook family plot. They had lived at Liberty Lake for many years, where he was a member of the Liberty Lake Community Church and the Elks Lodge #228.

Silas Cook's Sons

Warren Lawrence Cook, the elder son, fell ill at age five months with infantile paralysis, a disease later to be called "polio." There was little to be done for victims of this mysterious disease, but Warren survived. Medical costs for his parents were staggering in those days before the March of Dimes had been established. About 1960, Warren married Sandra Smith. They had one daughter born about 1964, but later divorced.

Warren became an impressive scholar. He received a doctorate in South American history with highest honors in Lima, Peru, and was fluent in Spanish, French, German and Portuguese. He spent many years in South America, including an expedition across the Andes and down the Amazon River. He was a D. Litt., Ph.D., Professor of History and Anthropology, a Fellow of the Epigraphic Society and was nominated for a Pulitzer Prize. His accomplishments and research skills are famous throughout the world of anthropology.

He became ill on a flight from New York to the home of his brother Charles in California. The plane landed in Omaha, Nebraska, where he was hospitalized and later died on December 7, 1989. His body was brought back to Spokane to be buried in the Cook family plot at Greenwood Memorial Terrace. His influence and fame will long continue.

Charles Edward Cook attended Washington State University before being called into the Navy during World War II, where he served as an air traffic controller in the Philippines. After the war he helped his parents with the roller skating rinks, where he met Patricia Hite, whom he married in 1949. He was involved in many enterprises during his life. He owned and operated the Five-Mile Ice Chalet, and he created an educational construction toy called the "D-Stix." He also published the *Northtown Star Shopper* for many years. He and his wife were active members of the First Presbyterian Church, where his grandparents, Francis and Laura Cook, had been charter members. He was also involved with the Campus Crusade For Christ.

Charles died on February 14, 2009, and was survived by his wife and their four sons: Charles "Skip" Jr., David, Richard W. and Steven D. He and Pat also had six grandchildren and eight great-grandchildren.

CLARA EMMA COOK
Fourth Child

Clara Emma was born January 12, 1887, in the first home in which her family lived on the South Hill. She was married November 15, 1906, to Hugh Leroy Fuson, who was born in Spokane on March 27, 1883. Clara died in December 1987, at the age of 100. Their children were: Francis Leroy Fuson, born in Spokane on January 12, 1910, and Lolita Ruth Fuson, born in Deer Park on March 18, 1913. Francis Fuson was married in Sacramento, California, June 28, 1940, to Aglaia Jouganatos and died in Las Vegas on February 12, 1992. Lolita "Corky" Fuson was married in San Francisco to George Walter Knight and died October 29, 2002, in Talent, Oregon. Prior to her death, Corky was an enthusiastic contributor of family information for this book.

Clara Emma Cook
(Photo courtesy Cook family)

Clara Cook lived a long and wonderful life and was a celebrity on her 100th birthday at the Mountain Vista Care Center in Talent, Oregon. Clara's interview with Louis Livingston is a goldmine of information about her parents and their life in the Spokane area. Her memories of the late 19th and early 20th centuries are an invaluable source for researchers today, and her recollection of the "big house" being built gives extraordinary proof of the location of the Francis Cook family in the 1880s and 1890s.

Clara remembered her childhood with pleasure. Her parents were loving but strict. If the children did anything that displeased her father, she recalled, "He never said anything to us. He just pulled his glasses down and looked at us *like that*, and that was all we needed." Most of her memories, however, were good ones. She recalled the children going hunting with their father—not for deer, however. She said, "Father would never kill a deer. He said there was something appealing about the face of a deer, that he could not shoot."

As she grew older, much of the responsibility for taking care of the younger children fell to her, as the older girls were then in high school. Clara was just ready to start high school when the last baby, Ralph, was born. Her parents took her out of school for that year to help her mother and the baby. When she finally went to high school, she boarded in Spokane with Judge and Mrs. Belt, her parents' friends. However, before she finished high school, when she was nineteen years old, she was married. Although she didn't actually speak about it, she implied there were some hard feelings between her and her parents for a while, probably because she married against their will.

She admitted she didn't particularly like the Mount Spokane project and also knew her mother wasn't happy about it either, because it kept Francis away from home. As always, however, Clara was understanding of her father. In speaking of his devotion to Mount Spokane, she said, "He loved it. He loved anything out in the open and he could see what it could be in the future for the residents of Spokane, which it did turn out that way. They came by the hundreds after the road was built and they were always up there."

She also had memories of her brothers and provided information about them that will be found in their biographies.

Clara and her husband, Hugh Fuson, remained good friends with her mother, and Clara told a lovely story about Laura Cook, long after Francis had died. Her mother said, "When I pass away, I want my pall-bearers to be my sons. Don't forget. Hugh is the one I love the most of all." What a nice tribute from a mother-in-law about her son-in-law!

Clara loved her husband too. "He was a wonderful, wonderful person," she said. They later moved to Klamath Falls, Oregon, in the 1940s. Hugh died in 1963, leaving Clara a widow for twenty-four years.

FRANK ARTHUR COOK
Fifth Child

Frank Arthur, the fifth child of Francis and Laura Cook and the second son, was born in Spokane on September 2, 1888 or 1889. His date of birth is in question. Army documents, driver's license, etc., give the date as 1889. However, a delayed birth certificate was issued (with the informant his sister Katharine Alvis), giving the date as 1888.

According to his World War I enlistment card, Frank worked as a service man for Yuba Manufacturing Company in Spokane, selling grading equipment before the war. In the 1918 *Spokane City Directory*, he is listed as living with his parents, the only time he is found in a directory. He joined the Army six months after the country entered the war and served as a master electrician at the Vancouver Barracks, Washington.

Frank Arthur Cook
(Photo courtesy Cook family)

On April 10, 1918, in Spokane, he married Helen Irma Cunningham, whom he had met while he was in service. She was born on October ber 17, 1890, in Minnesota, the daughter of Joseph E. and Mary Cunningham. Her father was a well-known builder in Spokane and was the contractor for several Spokane landmarks, including the original North Central High School, Holy Names Academy and the Hangman Creek Bridge. She and Frank had eight children, all born in Spokane: Edith Helen, Frances Patricia, James Edward, Frank Arthur Jr., John William, Thomas Woodward, Virginia Mary and Gwendolyn Joan.

Helen Cunningham Cook
(Photo courtesy Cook family)

After the war, Frank worked as a construction equipment salesman for Holt Manufacturing Company, which later merged with C. L. Best and became the Caterpillar Tractor Company. He traveled to many places, including South America. During the depression of the 1930s, they lost their home, which had

406. Latah Creek Bridge, 6th Ave., Spokane, Wash.
Length 1020 feet, Height 150 feet, 33,800 Cubic Yards of Concrete.
Cement supplied by the
LEHIGH PORTLAND CEMENT COMPANY
47,000 Barrels Used in the Construction

Hangman Creek Bridge, built by Helen Cook's father. *(Photo courtesy Cook family)*

been built by Helen's father, and moved to Milan, Washington, then later to Milwaukie, Oregon.

During World War II, Frank worked for Albina Shipyards in Portland as a welder, as did one of their daughters and a son. Two of Frank and Helen's sons served during World War II, one in the Navy and one in the Air Force. During this time in Portland, the oldest daughter died unexpectedly. Their youngest daughter had a lovely singing voice, and her daughter sang professionally for many years—another gift from Laura McCarty Cook.

After the war, the family returned to Deer Park, Washington, where Frank ran a welding shop, and then moved to Loon Lake, where he owned and operated a sawmill until his death. The youngest son served in the Air National Guard after the war and was killed in a motorcycle accident in 1950. At age 64, Frank died in Spokane on May 22, 1952, after suffering a stroke. He was the first of all the Cook children to die. Helen lived with one of her daughters until her death on May 10, 1962. Frank, Helen and other family members are buried at Spokane's Fairmount Memorial Park.

CHESTER ROBERT COOK
Sixth Child

Chester Robert, the third son of Francis and Laura Cook, was born in Spokane on July 12, 1890, in the house on the hill. He died in Eugene, Oregon, in February 1964. On February 4, 1908, in Coeur d'Alene, Idaho, he married Emma Laura Toombs, who was born in Seattle on December 13, 1892. Emma died in Eugene, Oregon, on August 22, 1979. The couple had a son, Chester R. Cook Jr., born about

1912. According to the 1920 Spokane census, they had another son, Gail Robert, born sometime in 1918.

Chester must have been one of the young sons who occasionally helped his father with the work on Mount Spokane. He is first found in the 1909 *Spokane City Directory*. By this time he was married, and the couple lived at 513 East Heroy. By 1910, he was employed by the "Cook Brothers." Actually, he was one of them, as he and brother Frank were operating a "wood" business of some sort. It apparently was not successful for long, as in later years Chester is listed as a carpenter, a teamster and an engineer.

Clara stated that at one time Chester went to Hollywood and worked in the movie studios. As a carpenter, he may have been adept at building stage sets, etc. In the 1920 and 1930 Spokane censuses, he is called a stage "electrician," so he definitely had some connection with the theatre.

Chester Robert Cook
(Photo courtesy Cook family)

There was a scarcity of archival information or family documents about Chester Cook and his family, and the above information was all that could be found.

EDITH LEE COOK
Seventh Child

Edith Lee was born in Spokane on February 2, 1892, in the house on the hill, and died in November 1980. She married Ralph Waldo Coblentz, who was born in Eldorado, Ohio, and died July 9, 1960, in Seattle. The couple had one daughter, Jean Coblentz, born about 1918 and died after 1937. Edith is found in the 1912 *Spokane City Directory*, boarding with her parents. In 1913, she was still living there and was an instructor at Pacific Telephone & Telegraph Company. In 1914, she was living at 1711 North Lidgerwood, still with the same company. This is where she met her husband, Ralph W. Coblentz, a salesman for the same company. Ralph was born in Ohio, where his father was a schoolteacher. By 1918, Ralph and Edith were living at 628½ South Howard. By this time, Ralph was a chief collector for the Home Telephone & Telegraph Company, located at Second Avenue and Stevens.

Edith Lee Cook
(Photo courtesy Cook family)

By the 1920 U.S. Census, the Coblentz family was living in Denver, Colorado, where Ralph was a traveling salesman. Their daughter Jean was born in Colorado, so Ralph and Edith must have left Spokane during 1918. In the 1930 census, the family was living in Tacoma, Washington.

LOLITA EVELYN COOK
Eighth Child

Lolita Evelyn was the eighth child and fifth daughter of Francis and Laura Cook. She was born in Spokane onovember 13, 1893, in the house on the hill. She died January 17, 1977, and is buried at Greenwood Memorial Terrace in Spokane.

Lolita attended the Cheney Normal School after high school, and in the fall of 1914, she began working as a teacher in Wilbur, Washington. Her sister Laura May Stookey and husband Frank were living in Wilbur at the time, so possibly Lolita was staying with them. Soon after, Lolita suffered a mental breakdown. She returned home to her parents, who admitted her to Medical Lake Hospital (now known as Eastern State Hospital) in February 1915. Lolita spent the next fifty-five years at the hospital, after which she was transferred to the Spokane Riverside Convalescent Home in 1970, where she died in 1977.

Burial plots were purchased by Francis and Laura and provision was made for Lolita to be buried with them. Charles Cook, Silas's son, followed their wishes and arranged for Lolita's burial in the family plot at Greenwood.

Lolita Evelyn Cook
(Photo courtesy Cook family)

Lolita's illness was devastating to her parents and siblings. Letters and family stories indicate that her brothers and sisters cared deeply for her, but the progression of her disease made it difficult to maintain a relationship. Her sister Clara named a daughter after her.

FLORENCE HELENE COOK
Ninth Child

Florence Helene was born in Spokane on November 26, 1896, the Cook's ninth child and the last baby born in the house on the South Hill. She died on January 1, 1997, in Concord, Contra Costa County, California. Florence was the most independent of the children. She left home as a young woman and went to Portland, Oregon, where she met her future husband Caesar DeBenedetti, a soldier who was stationed in Portland. He was born in Pacheco, California, on June 13, 1889.

Florence and Caesar (usually called "Deb") met before he was sent overseas during World War I. He was wounded, shot through the hand, and was first sent to San Diego. Later he was sent to the hospital in Portland. The couple was married on February 7, 1919, just three months after the signing of the Armistice, and they moved to California, where he worked for the Shell Oil Company. In addition, he operated a farm where he grew walnuts and grapes.

They had two children born in Oakland, California: Harold Burton, born March 7, 1920, and Warren Louis, born July 21, 1924. Caesar DeBenedetti was a Catholic, but according to Florence, he was not a strict Catholic. Florence's grandson, Michael, says that she attended a Presbyterian church at the corner edge of their farm. He describes her

**Florence Helene Cook
DeBenedetti**
(Photo courtesy Cook family)

as sincere and honest, but also strong-willed and stubborn, very much the matriarch of the family. At 96 years of age, she was still standing on a rickety ladder, picking "cots" from the apricot tree. Florence's husband died in Concord, California, in February 1969. Florence died there on January 1, 1997. Like her sister Clara, Florence lived to be 100 years old!

Caesar "Deb" DeBenedetti
(Photo courtesy Cook family)

Florence also was interviewed by Louis Livingston. According to John Ellingson, Livingston must have gone to California to meet with her, as the Livingstons often wintered in Arizona. She left wonderful memories of her parents and of her early life. She apparently was the most mischievous of the children and occasionally got into trouble. When asked by Livingston whether they had family devotions, she answered: "Father always asked the blessing and usually after he asked the blessing, I had done something naughty, and I *got the thumb* to leave the table."

As a married woman in California, she was the farthest away from the family and saw them rarely. She did remark that shortly after her first baby was born (March 7, 1920), she received a letter from her father, who was very ill by that time, saying he was getting better and hoped he would be able to come down and see "her little visitor." Francis never made it to California, as he died two months later.

WINIFRED JOSEPHINE COOK
Tenth Child

Winifred Josephine was born in Spokane County near Dartford on November 22, 1898, the first child born at the Cooks' Little Spokane property. She was married in Spokane on August 18, 1920, to Merle Hunt. Merle was born in Oregon on August 18, 1900, and lived for many years in St. John, Washington. Winifred was a cashier at the Davenport Hotel in 1918. In the 1920 St. John census, Merle is found as an assistant cashier. The couple was married shortly after the census was taken.

Winifred Cook
(Photo courtesy Cook family

While still in Spokane, Winifred and Merle had two children, Merle "Bud" and Patricia. By the 1930 census, the family was living in South Gate City, Los Angeles County, California, where Merle was a bank teller. Winifred died in California on July 8, 1985, and her ashes were sent to Spokane.

Nothing more has been found about the Cooks' last-born daughter. However, there is a typed record in the Cook collection that says: "Information furnished by Winifred Cook Hunt, January 7, 1981." It gives some basic information about her parents and the children, with their birthdates. But of more importance, there is a physical description of Francis H. Cook, which reads:

> Handsome man, well-trimmed side burns, stubborn, determined, high-principled. Children raised strictly. Used correct grammar, no slang or swearing; did not waste food (clean plates). Tall (6-feet), never carried a gun, but not afraid of anyone (including A. M. Cannon). Straight posture, full head of hair, always wore a black bow tie (even when fishing). A strong man.

She also gives a brief description of Laura McCarty Cook; "Red cheeks, curly hair, beautiful singing voice; called a 'spoiled doll' by her step-mother, and husband kept her so."

This is the only reference that says Laura had a "beautiful voice." It is interesting to note in the previous stories that several of Laura's descendants were also musically gifted.

RALPH WHEELER COOK
Eleventh Child

Ralph Wheeler, whose middle name came from Francis Cook's mother, was born on October 9, 1900, at the Little Spokane property, the last son and last child of Francis and Laura Cook. Ralph Cook was the baby of the family—not an easy position in a family of eleven children. However, he made his mark as Francis Cook's son. He had many good memories of the days on the Little Spokane and went to school at the little schoolhouse near Dartford. Ralph described his father as an "idealist" or "perfectionist." He was later to say: "He was fifty years ahead of people. He could see that far ahead."

Ralph Wheeler Cook
(Photo courtesy Cook family)

On December 9, 1918, in Spokane, he married Lillie Elizabeth Hansen, who was born January 19, 1900, in Snelling, Merced County, California, the daughter

Lillie Hansen Cook
(Photo courtesy Cook family)

of James Hansen and Anna Margaret Skow. Ralph and Lillie had one daughter, Doris Jean, born in Spokane on December 18, 1922. Doris Cook had a beautiful singing voice, possibly a legacy from her grandmother Laura McCarty Cook. In the 1930s, Doris often sang with well-known Spokane entertainer Cliff Carl. On August 4, 1942, she married Oscar "Ozzie" Bernard Hoffman, for twenty-seven years a member of the Spokane Police Department, retiring in 1973. The couple had three children: a daughter Laura Ann, another daughter Susan Elizabeth, and a son Paul Ralph. The two girls also inherited fine singing voices, so Laura Cook's legacy lived on. They often sang for special events in Spokane, at the Eagle's Lodge and other venues, and Laura sang with the "Up With People" chorus during Spokane's World's Fair, Expo '74. Laura Hoffman married Roger Poulin, who died in 2004, and Susan Hoffman married Dr. Bob Steadman. Both women still live in the Spokane area.

Ralph was possibly the closest to his father of all the children, as he lived with them at 614 East Wabash until his marriage. By 1919, he was called a "painter" in the *Spokane City Directory*. Later on, Ralph worked as a stagehand during the vaudeville era in Spokane and was a motion picture projectionist when "talkies" first came to town. A few years later, he became a truck driver and a farmer, and also raised registered Guernsey cattle on his farm near Eloika Lake.

He was a member of the Teamsters Union and Audubon Masonic Lodge. He was also an active supporter of the 4-H Club and the Future Farmers of America. He suffered a stroke in 1969 and died two years later. His obituary stated that he was survived by his wife, his daughter, three grandchildren and five sisters, including Lolita Cook of Spokane. Lillie lived for many years after her husband's death. Ralph and his wife, Lillie, are buried at Fairmount Memorial Park.

In his interview with Louis Livingston, Ralph was asked about his father's death. He replied, "Father had this terrible cancer, and they didn't do much for cancer at that time. They didn't do anything. They just listened to it until he died." When asked about his parents, he said, "They never did any fighting, and I can remember that. They never did any fighting that I know of when they were together."

This ends our account of the eleven children of Francis and Laura Cook. They were assuredly a diverse group of individuals, but they had in common an appreciation and admiration for their parents. There is evidence, repeatedly, that the children were raised in a strict but loving environment. They respected their mother and father, and their later lives reflect that upbringing. The three children who were interviewed in later life emphasize the kind of life that all the children experienced—a wonderful tribute to the two individuals who were responsible for them, Francis and Laura McCarty Cook.

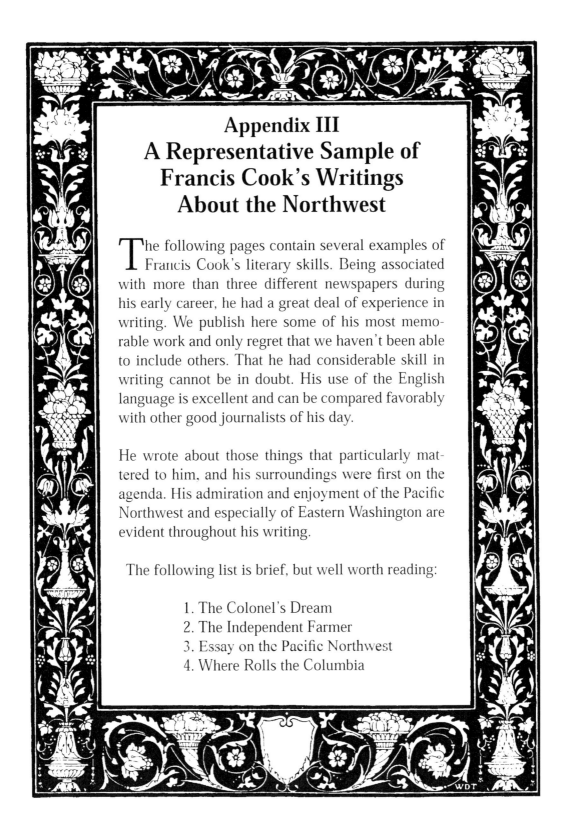

Appendix III
A Representative Sample of Francis Cook's Writings About the Northwest

The following pages contain several examples of Francis Cook's literary skills. Being associated with more than three different newspapers during his early career, he had a great deal of experience in writing. We publish here some of his most memorable work and only regret that we haven't been able to include others. That he had considerable skill in writing cannot be in doubt. His use of the English language is excellent and can be compared favorably with other good journalists of his day.

He wrote about those things that particularly mattered to him, and his surroundings were first on the agenda. His admiration and enjoyment of the Pacific Northwest and especially of Eastern Washington are evident throughout his writing.

The following list is brief, but well worth reading:

1. The Colonel's Dream
2. The Independent Farmer
3. Essay on the Pacific Northwest
4. Where Rolls the Columbia

THE COLONEL'S DREAM
by
Francis H. Cook

Who says he is not a renegade Sioux?
Who says he is a Spokane, tried and true?
    Me, and Curly Jim.

Who fought each other on field of the dead?
Who now are friendly like two in a bed?
    Me, and Curly Jim.

Who campaigned, real chummy,
   in times of yore?
Who battled bravely on the plains of gore?
    Me, and Curly Jim.

Who made the treaty on the Spokane plains?
Who signed it with their own magical names?
    Me, and Curly Jim.

Who allayed forever all scenes of strife?
Who brought peace and joy to pioneer life?
    Me, and Curly Jim.

Who supplied the Springfields
   in this wild land?
Who gave away guns with a lavish hand?
    Me, and Curly Jim.

Jim says, "I am a Skookum Boston man."
I say he's a *hyas tyee* Spokane –
    Me, and Curly Jim.

Now, we're gazing up at the deep blue sky,
To the happy hunting gounds – Jim and I.
We're longing to fly and I'll tell you why:
This sleepy old world is going too "dry."
    For me and Curly Jim.

That celestial sphere beats this one a mile;
For up there, once in a while, we get a "smile."
    Me, and Curly Jim.

We'll roam the heavens great sachems
   beguile;
As *tilakum ictas* were just the style,
    Me, and Curly Jim.

Then build a monument, good and high;
   Construct it so tall it will reach the sky.
Compel the good angels to wonder why
   The shaft for heroes is reaching so high,
Stretch it so high it can't go higher,
Dedicate it to those who must admire.
    Me, and Curly Jim.

James "Curly Jim" Silkoewoyeh. Most fittingly, in keeping with the last stanza of this poem, a monument was erected in Curly Jim's honor at Fairmount Memorial Park on September 13, 2006. *(Photo courtesy Spokane Public Library Northwest Room)*

THE INDEPENDENT FARMER

This poem was published in an early edition of the *Spokan Times*. It undoubtedly expressed his feelings about farming and the many people who embraced this type of life.

Let sailors sing of wind deep,
　　Let soldiers praise their armor,
But in my heart this boast I'll keep–
　　The independent farmer.
When first the rose, in robe of green,
　　Unfolds its crimson lining;
And round his cottage porch is seen
　　The honeysuckle climbing;
When banks of bloom their sweetness yield
　　To bees that gather honey,
He drives his team across the field,
　　When skies are soft and sunny.

The blackbird clucks behind the plows
　　The quail pines loud and clearly,
Yon orchard hides behind its boughs
　　The home he loves so dearly.
The gray and old barn doors unfold
　　His ample stores to measure,
More rich than heaps of hoarded gold
　　A precious, blessed treasure.
While yonder, in the porch, there stands
　　His wife, the lovely charmer,
The sweetest rose on all the lands -
　　The independent farmer.

To him the spring comes dancingly,
　　To him the summer blushes,
The autumn smiles with yellow ray,
　　His sleep old winter hushes.
He cares not how the world may move,
　　No doubts or fears confound him;
His little flock is linked in love,
　　And household angels round him.
He trusts to God and loves his wife,
　　Nor grief nor ills may harm her,
He's nature's nobleman in life–
　　The independent farmer.

(Photo courtesy Tony Bamonte)

THE PACIFIC NORTHWEST
by
Francis H. Cook

This essay was first printed in the *Spokan Times* on July 4, 1879, to provide the public with a description of Washington Territory, as Cook had viewed it on his cross-state tour the year before. It is interesting to note that Francis Cook was well aware of the distinct separation between Eastern and Western Washington. He had, by this time, been a resident of Olympia and New Tacoma, and had made the move to Spokane Falls. The essay was later edited by J. Orin Oliphant, a teacher at the Washington State Normal School, presently Eastern Washington State University, at Cheney, Washington. It is reprinted here as Mr. Oliphant transcribed it.

Mr. Oliphant concludes his introductory remarks with the following summation of Francis Cook:

> Cook belonged to that small class of unusual men whose vision leads them into enterprises for which the common lot of mankind is not ready. He was a promoter of worthy enterprises, but his enthusiasm induced him frequently to sponsor movements which were not at the time profitable. Time, however, has proved the worth of his faith, and those who came after him have gathered unto themselves the fruits of his foresight and prioneering labors. Francis H. Cook occupies in the annals of the Spokane country an honored place as one of its foremost builders.

NORTHWESTERN WASHINGTON

The Cascade mountain chain, extending north and south, and forming a dividing line between the eastern and western portions of Washington Territory, separates two distinctive climates, as well as two countries very dissimilar in points of topography and natural resources. Western Washington is, in the main, covered with a dense forest. Prairies are found, here and there, generally noted for sterility of soil and limited grazing fields. In no sense can Western Washington be called an agricultural country; although there are limited districts where the soil is very productive, and where farming can be carried on to advantage. Rivers, lakes, and mountain streams are very common to this portion of country.

The climate of Western Washington shows the most even temperature of any portion of the North Pacific Coast. The summer climate is delightful, and winter weather is scarcely ever too cold for rain. In fact, those persons who cannot be contented in a country where it is liable to rain much more than half the winter season, should choose the higher, dryer atmosphere found east of the

Early forest of Western Washington

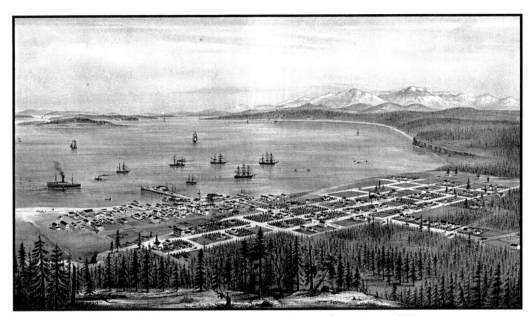

Bird's eye view of Port Townsend, situated on Puget Sound, in 1878. *(Library of Congress)*

Cascade mountains. We ought, perhaps, to state that the rainy weather of Western Washington is more of a continued drizzle, than storm, with about the same number of inches of rainfall during the year that visits the State of New York. Many people become used to this mild winter climate, and prefer it to any country whatsoever where the thermometer indicates colder winter weather. It is a noticeable fact that the winter climate of Western Washington is enjoyed by most persons who are situated so as to be within doors most of the time. Houses that have cracks in the outer walls large enough to put your hand through, are made comparatively comfortable by the mere use of enough fire to take the chill off. In too many instances, this mild climate encourages a lack of preparation for winter, and general shiftlessness, to such an extent that it occasions serious loss of health and property.

Puget Sound is the greatest or most remarkable feature in Western Washington. No one enters upon the waters of Puget Sound without being delighted with the scene, and astonished at the immensity of this little inland ocean. In no other portion of the world is there such an extensive harbor, where ocean vessels can lie in safety, along a shore line of fourteen hundred miles, and in the many bays which extend far into the interior from Puget Sound proper. All the sea-going vessels of the world permit our commercial relations to extend to all nations, as usual, with home and foreign vessels constantly entering into and departing from the various commercial and lumbering ports on the sound, without hindrance. Puget Sound varies, in width, from two to fifteen miles – except at the Narrows, a few miles above Tacoma, where the waters pass through between bluffs so near each other that from one shore a man can distinguish another on the opposite beach. The largest vessels afloat can enter upon and sail over Puget Sound in perfect safety. Experienced sea-going men inform us that Puget Sound is one of the calmest harbors in the world. Ordinary steamboats are making daily trips all over the Sound. Fish are obtained from these waters in great abundance. Clams are a staple product, where the beach is sandy, and when the tide has ebbed. The tides rise and fall some sixteen feet, twice each day.

Lumbering interests on Puget Sound are very extensive. The manufacture of lumber here is carried on in a most thorough manner. The best and truest machinery is used. We might name mills on the Sound that cut from 60,000 to 120,000 feet in a single day's run. Vessels are loaded with lumber and spars, at Puget Sound ports, and sail for various foreign countries. For ship-building purposes, the fir of Puget Sound is probably unequalled for length, strength and durability. Future years will develop the importance of Puget Sound in the matter of ship-building. The chief wealth of Western Washington, in years past, has been its immense forests.

An early logging train on the West Coast. *(Library of Congress)*

The mining resources of Puget Sound are being developed, and this unmeasured field of wealth promises an abundant harvest in Western Washington. Gold and silver are found in many localities, in limited quantities. Lead and copper abound in the Cascade mountains, especially in and about Mount Rainier. This mountain peak stands in the eastern end of Pierce county, and lifts its snow-covered peak 14,440 feet above the level of the sea. The view from New Tacoma, looking toward this mountain, is very imposing. Nothing is gathered from beneath the earth's surface, in the wilds of Western Washington, that yields a handsome profit, except coal. Within the last four or five years, the working of coal mines has become one of the most important industries in Western Washington. The most promising mines are now located at Seattle and Puyallup Valley, the latter a few miles from New Tacoma. The former mines yield some six hundred tons of coal per day. The products of the Tacoma Colliery are destined, in future, to figure largely in the principal coal marts along the Pacific's shores.

Immigration to Western Washington occasions a gradual increase in population. The farming lands of this section of country are very productive. Here, all ordinary field crops are raised, except such as corn, melons and grapes; and even those may be grown in limited quantities. Farming operations on Puget Sound are attended with much hard labor, owing to the heavy growth of timber and underbrush on most of the best lands. In the matter of agriculture, most farmers are best pleased in Eastern Washington, where farming operations are carried on with much less difficulty than in thickly timbered countries.

The principal towns in Western Washington are: Port Townsend, the American port entry to Puget Sound; Seattle, the leading business center; Olympia, the Territorial capital; and the Tacomas, where are located the Tacoma sawmill and the terminus of the Northern Pacific Railroad. Seattle has a population of some 3,500 souls; Olympia, about 2,000. In the event of the completion of the N.P.R.R. to Puget Sound—which is not an improbability—New Tacoma promises to become a very important commercial point. Her granaries will then be receptacles of the harvests of Eastern Washington, and her warehouses will receive the imports from, and the exports for various foreign countries. Years hence, other points on the railroads and telegraph lines are already well represented in Western Washington. School and church privileges are enjoyed in all towns along the shores of Puget Sound, and in some of the more important settlements. Newspapers are published in abundance. The general intelligence of the people of Puget Sound is above the average. Clerks, common laborers, and persons "waiting for something to turn up," are much more numerous than desirable situations. There are industries undeveloped which might be inaugurated with profit, by persons who have capital and good business qualifications.

NORTHEASTERN WASHINGTON

There is probably no country now known to the American people, the name of which sounds so pleasantly upon the ear of the homeless and unsettled as that of Northeastern Washington. Only distance from the more densely populated countries, prevents Eastern Washington from becoming, in a single season, a very populous region. For years and years after the discovery of this great country, the green grass waved over an almost pathless meadow; the waters of the Spokan thundered through an uninhabited region; and nature, clothed in the habiliments of promised wealth and surpassing grandeur, remained unadorned and unappropriated. But, as the restless wave of immigration pressed its way across the American Plains; swept over the Rocky Mountains; and finally, rested upon the Pacific's peaceful shore, the curiosity of the most curious brought a very few families into the country now known as Northeastern Washington.

The earliest settlers here only hoped to find a grazing field for stock; a veritable "home in some vast wilderness;" or a simple retreat from more densely populated countries. Time and the tide of emigration, however, wait for nothing. While the one speeds stealthily, noiselessly on, the other sails over seas, sweeps over continents, and populates a nation.

The dozens who first came to the North Pacific Coast were soon followed by hundreds; the hundreds, by thousands; and the thousands, by tens of thousands. Every considerable tide of emigration is accompanied or soon followed by capital and wisdom. When pioneer families suffered the discomforts, and dared the dangers, of a long and tiresome journey across the continent, and were perfectly satisfied with the haven they had found in the Pacific Northwest, men of capital began to inquire more earnestly into the merits of this great country. It became thoroughly known that, aside from the mining interests that were being developed at an early day, the immense forests of superior timber on Puget Sound, and the great meadow lands of Eastern Washington would encourage and support a large population in the future. By referring to maps, and through earnest inquiry, regarding ocean currents and prevailing winds, it became evident that very important commercial centers in the East could be reached more easily from Puget Sound than from any other American port. The flood of emigration steadily continued from the Atlantic to the Pacific.

The happy idea of uniting the East with the West terminated in the completion of the Union and Central Pacific railroad across the continent, the greatest internal achievement known to the history of nations. But that line did not suffice to satisfy the demands of a rich and rapidly developing country in the northern and western portions of the United States. Preliminary surveys demonstrated the feasibility of a trans-continental railroad route several hundred miles north of the Union and Central Pacific road, where snows are less prevalent, and through a richer and better country. Shrewd capitalists took in the situation at once, and offered to assist in pushing the proposed line of the Northern Pacific to successful completion. the Great Lakes of the Atlantic seaboard were to be united with Puget Sound. Mistakes in the early management, and errors in the judgment, displayed by the N.P.R.R. Co., together with general financial depression all over the country, checked, for the time-being, growing sentiment which had sprung up in favor of this great enterprise. But the demand for the road remained unsatisfied; and the gigantic project assumed a more tangible shape,

The town and the Spokane River as it appeared in 1883, shortly after Francis Cook moved to Spokane. *(Photo from Mark Danner's Patsy Clark Album. courtesy Tony and Suzanne Bamonte)*

Celebrating the joining of the Northern Pacific Railroad tracks from the east and the west at Gold Creek, Montana, on September 8, 1883. *(Public domain photo)*

and again became a theme of national interest and public solicitude. Its prospects became brighter; its friends grew more numerous; and rival interests more defiant, because it gave promise of becoming a grand success. In hopes of reaping some of the benefits which are generally derived from the construction of a railroad through a new and naturally immense country, immigration to the Pacific Northwest has become a matter of general comment all over our nation. Owing to fertility of soil, a delightful climate, and an almost unlimited quantity of available government lands, coupled with promises of early railroad connection with Puget Sound and the East, Northeastern Washington has become a new Eldorado of America--the most inviting haven for those who are wanting to locate in a new and growing country. From the West, the South and the East, immigrants come pouring into Northeastern Washington. They pitch their tents upon the broad prairies; build their houses along the timbered line; settle upon tracts of rich prairie soil in the midst of forests; dwell upon the highly productive mountain slopes; or feed their herds and flocks upon the green pastures of an almost limitless expanse.

WHITMAN and STEVENS COUNTIES

Whitman and Stevens Counties combine to make up that important section of country known as Northeastern Washington. Together, they unite in the formation of a most beautiful country. Inseparably connected, and delightfully intermingled, are their hills and valleys, plains, forests and running streams, which constitute this wonderful region. Sunshine and a genial clime are characteristics not to be forgotten. Every breeze, as it sweeps over the beautiful landscape, purifies itself by running streams, in vast areas of waving grass, and amid the burly pines and other forest trees. The herder drives his flocks over rolling prairies, until, fatigued with eating, they lie down in green pastures and rest. Hunters pursue retreating game up into the dizzy heights, and gather food from forest glades. The farmer guides his plow over a gradually undulating plain, turning an even sod; and the rich virgin soil brings forth its first harvest in abundance. Already, issuing smoke from the camp-fire, the tent, and the home of the settler, arises from every important valley and plain; the embryo of a great populace takes its shape. Surely, this is a promising land of comfort. Providence has scattered its choicest gifts, with a plentiful hand, over this beautiful country. Nature, lavish in the bestowal of its greatest benefits, has charmed the eye of man by the grandeur of the landscape, and taught us to consider with pleasure the wonderful works of God. Golden harvests measure the intrinsic worth of this soil. Health wreathes

Early harvesting operation in the Palouse. *(Photo from the Marshall Shore Collection)*

its pleasant impress into every feature of the human countenance. In this delightful clime pleasure is sought after and found by those who know best how to enjoy it. The influence of the genial climate, and pleasant surroundings, are alike comforting and beneficial. Even the cheerfulness of the morning sun, and its pleasant influences, find a counterpart in the whole-souled, good-natured people who dwell in this land.

Were we asked to indicate one of the prettiest spots on earth, where climate, soil and topographical elements are most congenial to health and present prosperity, we could not do otherwise than refer, without hesitancy, to the great Spokan country. Man has scarcely dreamed, in his most extravagant fancies, of an ideal country which has not a counterpart in the vicinity of the Spokan. Does he desire a rich soil? If so, he may gather abundant harvests about the Four Lakes, White Bluff Prairie, Deep Creek, Crab Creek, Rock Creek, and in various other highly favored sections. Is he fond of sporting? Is so, he should gather satisfaction from these hills and forests; launch his barque upon the beautiful Coeur d'Alene and Pend Oreille lakes, which are respectively thirty and sixty miles in length. Fish are abundant in these waters; and here lake trout often attain to ten and twelve pounds each in weight. Waterfowl and prairie chickens are here quite plentiful, in their season. Does he love excellent roads? The natural drives on the Spokan plains are probably unequaled in the world. They are remarkable for their evenness, and for freedom from either dust or mud. One may be an ardent admirer of a variety of scenery, We would gratify his curiosity. Here he may ascend to a dizzy mountain height, and, from one position, look admiringly down upon hills, valleys and plains, forests, groves and sparsely timbered sections, rich soil and gravelly prairies, pleasant homes and forest fastnesses, the mirror-like lake and the roaring torrent of the wonderful Spokan, trackless glades and level roads, barren, rocky cliffs, and green verdure and blossoming vegetation, unadorned nature, and promising harvests, the beautiful and the grand.

COLVILLE VALLEY

One of the oldest settlements in Eastern Washington is that which owes its early existence to the establishment of a fort, by the Hudson's Bay Company, in the country now known as Colville Valley, situated in Northeastern Washington. This beautiful valley is about sixty-five miles long, and has a width varying from one to two miles. The valley is well timbered, and is surrounded by forest of fir, tamarack, birch, maple, cedar, and black, white and yel-

Near the site of the old Fort Colvile, the Hudson's Bay Company fur-trading post on the Columbia River. *(Photo courtesy Stevens County Historical Society)*

An old homestead in the Colville Valley. *(Photo courtesy Stevens County Historical Society)*

low pine. Trees here grow more lofty, and produce a clearer and better quality of lumber, than any other forest in Eastern Washington (with, perhaps, the exceptions known to exist about Coeur d'Alene and Pend Oreille Lakes). Delightful prairie lands contribute to the beauty and natural wealth of Colville Valley. The soil varies, from a rich vegetable mold to heavy, productive clay. Grazing in and about Colville Valley has been most excellent in years gone by. Large herds of stock are no longer kept here with profit. However, the farmer who has from ten to twenty head of stock to pasture upon the commons, has to feed but lightly during the year; principally, he feeds during winter and spring months.

The course of Colville Valley lies north and south. Near midway between the ends of the valley there is a lake, from which the Colville river takes its source, running northward and emptying into the Columbia; and the Chemekain, running southwest, and emptying into the Spokan. During the months of May, June, July, August and September, this country is said to be a delightful field for the tourist and sportsman. Fish abound in the streams; duck, geese and brant are quite plentiful; and deer are said to be easily captured in the forests.

Haying in the Colville Valley. *(Photo courtesy Stevens County Historical Society)*

WHERE ROLLS THE COLUMBIA
by
Francis H. Cook

The mighty Columbia River. *(Photo courtesy Library of Congress)*

Starting where the Rocky Mountains rise,
Where snowy pinnacles pierce the skies;
Warmed into life by the sun's bright rays,
Increasing size where the warm wind strays,
Dashing and dancing down the steep hill,
Beginning a sparkling, splashing rill,
   Where's born the Columbia.

Only a little bright rill at first,
Just a tiny streamlet that burst
Into the sunshine, out of the shade,
Kissing the glaciers, hiding in glade;
Starting in peaks of eternal snow,
Far to the west it ever must flow,
Following the course it always ran
From earliest days, when the world began,
   Where rolls the Columbia.

This babbling brook, with increasing length,
Gains width and depth and size and strength,
As down the mountain side it gushes,
And through the narrow gorges rushes
Into the tortuous riverbed
That first is seen on this watershed.
   Where rises the Columbia.

Enlarged by every merging brook
That rushes wild from valley and nook,
And gathering from each sparkling stream
New lease of active life, 'twould seem
The river here has fairly begun
The long, long journey it has to run
'Tween rocky peaks that kiss the skies
And Pacific's shores where billows rise,
   Where rolls the Columbia.

Rushing down through mountains cold and
    bleak
Still on through woodlands, rough and wild
And into civilization mild;
Under the strong iron track which spans
From sea to sea these wonderful lands.
Then merging into a broadening lake
Where Indians once were wont to make
In glad times of yore, when wild and free
Their journeys over this inland sea.
        Where glides the Columbia.

Slowly and gently gliding along
Is this land of poetry and song,
Baring her bosom to business strife,
Feeling the pulse of commercial life;
Borne on the beautiful Arrow lakes;
Converging, the water once more makes
A mighty river, grand in its mien,
A glistening gem in this bright scene,
        Where rolls the Columbia.

Flowing on in a southerly course,
It moves with irresistible force,
King Edward's bonds so soon to sever,
And leaves Canadian soil forever;
Joins America's land of the free,
And onward wends its way to the sea,
        Where rolls the Columbia.

Glorious Columbia! Pride of the west!
Draining a land that ranks with the best;
Joining with rivers we all admire,
Traveling through the Inland Empire;
This peerless land of wonderful yields
Rich mines, luscious fruits and golden fields,
Where people prosper, contentment reigns,
In cities, towns and homes of the plains
        Where rolls the Columbia.

Rushing onward, as in times of yore,
Reaching out for the Oregon shore,
Then turning again to the westward, ho!
As madly its foaming waters go
Through narrow canyons, rocky and wild,
Then spreading out broadly, calm and mild,
It trends through scenes of historic lore
Sacred to all this Northwestern shore,
        Where rolls the Columbia.

Down through the gorge in Cascade
    mountains
Dashing waters and tumbling fountains
Foam in riverbed, sparkle in hills,
Disclosing scenic splendor the thrills,
The passing on through mountain of snow
That over towering hilltops show;
And bordered by everlasting green,
All lending to this enchanting scene
A riverview grandeur unsurpassed
Where Hudson's scenery is outclassed,
        Where rolls the Columbia.

Onward, westward, this grand river flows
Wider, deeper, majestic it grows;
Floating vessels with bunting unfurled
That haul our goods to the wide, wild world,
Teeming with business from every land,
And bounded by wealth on either hand,
        Where rolls the Columbia.

Ceaselessly flowing to the west,
Meeting the ocean's white-coated crest,
Ending at last its race to the sea,
Its course being run, only to be
Buried beneath the great billows deep,
There forever, evermore to sleep
Under a winding shroud, that unfurled,
Reaches around this wonderful world,
        Where ends the Columbia.

EPILOGUE

Francis Cook truly loved his adopted home in Eastern Washington. It is evident in many things he did, but never more so than in the above poem. Before coming to Spokane, he had traveled all the land between the coast and Idaho so he knew what he was writing about.

Sources

Bamonte, Tony and Suzanne Bamonte. *Manito Park, A Reflection of Spokane's Past*. Spokane, Wash: Tornado Creek Publications, 1998.

Belshaw, Maria Parsons and George Belshaw. "Journey from Indiana to Oregon, Journal of George Belshaw." *Crossing the Plains to Oregon in 1853*. Fairfield, Wash: Ye Galleon Press, 2000.

Cook family papers, pictures and letters. Furnished by Francis Cook's great-granddaughters Jan Fray Edmonds and Laura Hoffman Poulin, granddaughter Lolita "Corky" Fuson Knight, and grandson Burton Alvis.

Cook, Charles A. "Pioneering Reminiscences in the United States Vast Area for Nearly a Century." Typescript. No date.

Cook, Laura McCarty. Personal papers. Northwest Museum of Arts & Culture (MAC). MsSC50.

Cook, Silas (father of Francis H.) Patent No. 5,276 United States Patent Office. Reissued February 11, 1873.

Daughters of the American Revolution Records. Catharine Ford Cook. #2974.

Deed Books. Archives of the Spokane County Auditor. Spokane County Courthouse, Washington.

Dorpat, Paul and Jean Sherrard. *Washington Then & Now*. Tacoma, Wash: Westcliffe Publishers, 2007.

Edwards, Jonathan. *An Illustrated History of Spokane County, State of Washington*. San Francisco: W. H. Lever, 1900.

Fort Harmar, Ohio. Online at <http://www.ohiohistorycentral.org>.

Glover, James N. *Reminiscences of James N. Glover*. Fairfield, Wash: Ye Galleon Press, 1985.

Graham, Bernice and Elizabeth S. Cottle. *Washington County (Ohio) Marriages 1789-1840*. Baltimore, Maryland: Genealogical Publishing Co., 1976.

Hatcher, Patricia Law. *Producing A Quality Family History*. Salt Lake City: Ancestry, Inc., 1996.

History of Washington County, Ohio, 1789-1881. Sponsored by the Washington County Historical Society, Marietta, Ohio. H. Z. Williams & Bro. Publishers, 1881.

Hunt, Charles W. *History of Harrison County, Iowa; Its People, Industries and Institutions*. LaCrosse, Wisconsin: Brookhaven Press, ca. 2000.

Hunt, Herbert. *History of Tacoma, Washington*. Vol. I: 1852-1890. 1916. Reprint. Tacoma: Tacoma Historical Society Press, 2005.

Jensen, Derrick and George Draffan. *Railroads and Clearcuts: Legacy of Congress's 1864 Northern Pacific Railroad Land Grant*. Spokane, Wash: Public Lands Council, 1995.

The Kincaid Story. Published by the Sumner Historical Society, 1991.

Lewis, Robert. *Handbook of American Railroads*. New York City: Simmons-Boardman Publishing Co., 1956.

Naches Pass Wagon Trail Marker. Online at <http:\\www.waymarking.com/waymarks/>.

Newspapers
      Daily Ledger (Tacoma, Washington), March 6, 1889
      Northwest Tribune (Cheney, Washington), various issues
      Pierce County Herald, February 18, 1876.
      Seattle Times, December 31, 1961.
      Spokane Chronicle, various issues
      Spokane Falls Review, various issues
      Spokan Times, various issues
      Spokesman-Review, various issues
      Tacoma Daily News, various issues
      Wilbur (Washington) *Register*
      Yakima Daily Republic/Yakima Morning Herald

Oliphant, J. Orin. Introduction to *The Territory of Washington, 1879*, by Francis H. Cook. Cheney, Wash: Reprinted by the State Normal School, Cheney, Washington, 1925.

Oral histories conducted by Louis Livingston, transcribed by John Ellingson, 1987. Northwest Museum of Arts & Culture/Eastern Washington State Historical Society, Spokane, Washington. Clara Cook Fuson: OH-789; Florence Cook DeBenedetti: OH 788; and Ralph Wheeler Cook: OH 790.

Pierce County, Washington, Marriage Records.

Pierce County, Washington. *Thumbnail History*. Online at <HistoryLink.org).

Polk, R. L. *Spokane City Directories*. Spokane, Wash: all available years 1889-1930.

Price, Lori and Ruth Andersoon. *Puyallup, Washington: Pioneer Paradise*. Charleston, South Carolina: Arcadia Publishers, 2002.

Records of Fairmount Memorial Cemetery, Greenwood Memorial Terrace, and Riverside Memorial Park. Spokane, Washington.

Stricker, Clyde Thomas. *Purchasing A Mountain*. Spokane, Wash: Published by the author, 1975.

Thimsen, Blythe. "Spokane's Loose Cannon: A. M. Cannon's Impact on Spokane." *Spokane Coeur d'Alene Living*. June 2009. pp. 80-84.

United States Department of Agriculture. *Naches Pass Historical Trail*. Forest Service, Pacific Northwest Region.

United States Federal Censuses, 1830 through 1930.

United States Works Projects Administration, Washington (State). *Told By The Pioneers*. Olympia, Wash: 1937-1938.

Washington County, Ohio, Marriage Records, Vol. 1 & 2.

Washington County, Ohio. Probate Records, W-1823 & 1832.

Washington State and Territorial Censuses: 1857, 1879 and 1895.

White, Virgil S. *Genealogical Abstracts of Revolutionary War Pension Files*, Vol. 4. Waynesboro, Tenn: 1991. File #W-26002, Samuel Wheeler, Connecticut Line, page 3772.

INDEX

Medical Lake Hospital 103
Meeker, Ezra 88-89
Mertz, Peter 43, 45
    chief of police 41
    streetcar conductor 41
Meserve, Jane 74
Mining resources 113
Mirror Lake 50, 52
Money, Mr. and Mrs. 9
Montrose development 47
Montrose Park 38, 40, 50, 52
Moore, F. R. 20
Morning Review
    fair 36-37
    motor line 40
Morris, Amy 96
Moses, Col. A. Benton 88
Motie, Marguerite
    "Miss Spokane" 63,
    65-66
Motorized streetcar line 38
Mount Carlton
    also called "Mount
    Baldy" 59, 63
Mount Rainier 6-7
Mount Spokane 1-2, 60, 99
    christening 63-68
    map 63, 67
    sale of land 69
    surveying 61
Museum of Arts and Culture
    (MAC) 91
Muskingum River 72

N

Naches Trail 84
Nelson, Ed 43
New Tacoma, Washington
    [*see* Tacoma,
    Washington]
New York Tribune 4
Newspapers 2, 5-7, 9, 11-12,
    15, 17-18, 20-21,
    24-25, 27-31, 33-34,
    36-37, 40-41, 56,
    59-60, 68, 82, 85,
    93-94, 98
Nishinomiya, Japan
    sister city 54
Nishinomiya Japanese Garden
    origin of 54
Nishinomiya-Tsutakawa
    Japanese Garden 54
North Central High School
    100
North Pacific Times 9, 12
Northeasterm Washington
    Colville Valley 120
    description of 15, 116

Northeastern Washington
    (continued)
    Palouse country 118
    Palouse harvesting 118
    Spokane plains 118
    Fort Colville 119
Northern Pacfic Railroad
    7-9, 11-12, 19, 39,
    55, 79, 116-117
    criticized by Cook 9
Northtown Star Shopper 98
Northwest Magazine 42, 45
Northwest Tribune 20, 24
    assault on Cook 27, 29
    fair 37
Northwestern & Pacific
    Hypotheekbank 50

O

Odell, Julia 76
Ogden, Elizabeth 93
Old Baldy 59, 63
Oliphant, J. Orin
    description of Francis
    Cook 112
Olympia Echo 5-6
Olympia, Washington 3-4,
    6-7, 112, 115
Oregon State Navigation Co.
    8, 12

P

Pacific Northwest
    description of 112-116
Pacific Telephone &
    Telegraph Co. 102
Palouse Gazette 15
Panic of 1893 47-49
    described 49
Parsons, Sarah 86
Peebles, Cad 40
Pend Oreille Lake 11
Pierce County, Washington
    12
    schools 87
Port Townsend, Washington
    112, 115
Porter, John D. 62
Portland Oregonian 7
Portland Standard
    assault on Cook 28
Poulin, Laura Hoffman 107
Poulin, Laura McCarty 14
Poulin, Roger 107
Provident Trust Co. 38, 50
Public land [*see* Land grants]
Puget Sound Courier 5
Puget Sound, Washington 7,

Puget Sound *(continued)*
    113-117
Puyallup, Washington 85

R

Railroads
    Northern Pacific 8-9, 11
    Oregon State Navigation
    Co. 8
    Union & Central Pacific
    Railroad 116
Reservoir 45-46
Review building 22
Revolutionary War 71-73, 76
Ring, The 24-25
Riverside Memorial Park 44,
    69, 97
Rockwood addition 41
Ross, A. J. 39
Routhe, E. A. 38

S

Sacred Heart Hospital 38
Shakespeare, William 1
Shannon, Bill 39
Sherman, Marjorie Cook 83
Shore, Marshall Belshaw 86
Silkoewoyey, James "Curly
    Jim" 110
Simmons, L. W. 87
Simmons, Mary McCarty 87
Simonson, John 39
Sisters of Charity 5
South Central High School
    43
South Hill property 32
Spirit Lake 60
Spokan Times 2, 11, 15,
    20-21, 31, 111-112
    accomplishments 24
    assault on Cook 26-27
    building 15, 17, 19, 25,
    93, 96
    Francis H. Cook poem
    111-112
    location of 15, 17, 19
    sale of 30, 33, 94
Spokane & Montrose Motor
    Railroad 38-39
    car barns 38
    electrification 41
    first motor streetcar 38
    first steam engine 43
    improvements 51
    route of 38, 42
    trial trip 40
Spokane Chamber of
    Commerce 62-63